MORE THAN AN ADVENTURE

"Help From the Air Makes It There"–The Unusual Adventures of Helimission

by Hedi Tanner

More Than an Adventure - Helimission
ISBN 1-59919-007-9
Copyright © 2006 Hedi Tanner

Scripture quotations taken from the King James
Version of the Holy Bible.

First English edition 2006
Translated by: Anke Stoye

Printed in the United States of America

German Original
Title of the German original:
Mehr als ein Abenteuer – Die ungewöhnliche Arbeit
der Helimission

ISBN 3-85645-059-9
Best.-Nr. 307059
4. Auflage 2003
© 1989 by Dynamis Verlag, CH-8280 Kreuzlingen
Umschlaggestaltung: Ernst Tanner/bix-grafik
Gesamtherstellung: Schönbach-Druck GmbH,
Erzhausen

Printed in Germany

I have decided...

to believe,
to love,
to act.

Albert Schweitzer

Contents

Preface

In this high-tech day and age, we as Christians have to take a good, long, hard look at ourselves and ask the uncomfortable question: "Do we really still need pioneers in the fields of evangelism and missions today?" Those living on fairly safe and comfortable terrain in the Western World might deny this categorically. Before dismissing the issue completely, it might be wise to do some traveling to India or Africa or South America and get in touch with the Third World. There, you come face to face with a time warp of decades, if not centuries, as far as technological development is concerned. This means that yes, pioneers are vital to Christian missions, even today.

Ernst "Ernie" Tanner is one such pioneer. Apprehended by the love of God, he initially makes a decision to serve his own countrymen in Switzerland. While touring Africa, he soon discerns the hidden cry of unreached tribes, villages and regions. This cry becomes a commission which does not let go of him, even back in Europe. He embarks upon a reckless adventure in faith.

In reading the upcoming pages, you will feel yourself drawn into this risky undertaking for God. You may find yourself involuntarily holding your breath at times. The suspense is nearly tangible. You will experience the fears, disappointments, defeats and victories of this dedicated man of God and his family.

During the course of history, God has always been looking for people to trust Him completely. These are people who defy all human reasoning and have the courage to follow His instructions completely. At times, it may seem more than you can take, but God is far greater than any challenge in our way. Ernie Tanner and his entire family are living proof, having experienced His faithfulness firsthand.

It is my privilege and honor to have been a participant in this moving story. My heartfelt desire for everyone reading this is to receive fresh inspiration through this book. May you be spurred on to renew your trust in a God Who is ever-present, ever-living and ever-working on your behalf.

Erich Theis

Part One

Chapter 1

Big Brother

The summer heat lay like a stifling blanket over the large industrial city. The asphalt surface of the road had gone soft, shimmering under the red-hot sky.

On the woody edge of town, Jack stopped on his way home. He took in a deep breath of the cool air wafting toward him from the shady path. The trees beckoned him to come further into the green forest. He let out a sigh, lingering a moment to enjoy it. This was home. He knew every tree and every bush here. These were *his* trees and *his* bushes. They were his native stomping grounds. On his nature expeditions, he had often stumbled across animals by surprise. Watching these four-footed friends at close range was, to him, one of life's greatest pleasures.

The stillness of the woods engulfed him. The silence held a sort of magic for him. Yet, today things seemed too quiet. Was it the overwhelming heat? All at once, he perked up, listening with all his faculties. What was that sound coming from the woods? Was someone calling? Everything got quiet again. Then, he heard yells coming from the east. His whole body tensed up. Then, like an Indian on moccasins, he began racing through the trees.

There they were again, those screams in the distance. That was a child crying for help! Wild thoughts darted through his mind. He could still manage to hear a sound, this time, a stifled sob. By now, he was barely touching the ground, light as a feather, trying to keep from making any kind of sound. Then, he heard other voices...first, one child crying...then another one. A male voice was laughing. What on earth was going on?

As he gingerly moved from cover to cover, the voices grew louder and louder. He heard groaning and then laughter. In between, someone bellowed out commands. Jack hit the ground, crawling cautiously closer. Like a snake, he crept inch by inch through the leaves. He was hardly breathing. No one should hear him! He wanted to make out what the voices were saying. The crying got louder as did the haughty, scornful laughter.

At last, he recognized a figure at the upper edge of the woods. A big boy kneeling on the ground was occupied with something or someone. A hilly mound in the soil blocked Jack's view. Just a few more inches...then he could see. He lifted his head slowly. What he saw made him stop breathing. A whole group of boys, younger and older ones, were sitting on top of kids they had tied up. They were "torturing" their whimpering, dirt-covered victims.

Then, Jack noticed the cows grazing down in the valley, thinking, "Aren't those the neighbor's cows?" Immediately, everything was clear. School was off for the afternoon. The neighbor's children had joined a farm worker in bringing the cattle to the meadow. Then, they had wanted to spend the afternoon there. The "city slickers," a group of boys who were at loggerheads with Jack, had overcome the kids and tied them up. The young farmhand, helpless and speechless, stood over to the side.

Suddenly, Jack heard a "battle cry" from behind him. He jumped to his feet. At once, he found himself surrounded by a bunch of "soldiers," armed with clubs, slingshots and ropes. Fully absorbed by the plight of the screaming kids, he had overlooked the tents on the other side of the valley. From there, the lookouts had crept up on him unnoticed.

Now the others left their victims and came rushing over. For a couple of seconds, Jack stood there unsure of what to do, surrounded by rods and whips. No one yet dared approach him because Jack was much bigger than they, though hardly older than the biggest of them. Jack whirled around in the direction of the woods. He put his fingers to his mouth and whistled with all of his might. All heads turned in the same direction to see to whom he was whistling. At that second, Jack dashed past his circle of enemies at full speed. The others were too stunned to follow.

Out of breath and drenched in sweat, he reached home. Right away he called for his younger brother "Ent" to meet him in the basement. He grabbed an axe and worked the end of a piece of wood into a round handle. Meanwhile, still trying to catch his breath, he filled his brother in. Then he reached for a second piece of wood for him. Jack was furious at those despicable boys. Driven partly out of vengeance and partly by a desire to free the neighbors' kids, they hurried back to the woods.

The trees seemed to be moving with them as they ran at top speed. The tension mounted with every step. Within a matter of minutes, they had reached their destination. They stood still, remaining undercover, trying to listen. Every now and then, they could hear a scream.

The area was no longer being watched. Apparently no one was expecting Jack back. In order not to be noticed again by those on the other side, the two crawled from tree to tree, from cover to cover. Soon they were only a few feet away. There had to be between ten and fifteen boys, which meant the others certainly had the upper hand.

Jack and Ent looked each other in the eye. A solemn handshake followed. Then, shouting at the top of their lungs, they fell upon the torturers. It all happened so fast that the biggest among them, probably the leader, did not have time to get up. With arms outstretched, Jack flew upon his neck, knocking him to the ground. Number Two toppled at the same moment. Ent followed up with Number Three. In no time at all, Jack was back on his feet, pursuing the fellows running away, who simply left their victims behind. In the meantime, Ent untied two of the kids. They, in turn, helped the others. Then all of them ran down the mountain, following their heroes.

The first ones to flee had already reached the street below the meadow. The last ones could barely muster up the strength to get on their feet and go. Thoroughly

shaken, the lookouts packed up their tents and fled to the
street. That was the unofficial meeting point. Only then
did they realize whom they had been running away from
– just two Tanner boys. How degrading! Clenching their
fists, they yelled for Jack to come back. Of course, neither
he nor Ent had any intention of returning. Instead, they
let out a victory shout. Their little friends joined in. Jack,
Ent and the neighbors' kids then returned to the village,
all puffed up like peacocks. There, they relished telling
their buddies all about their incredible adventure.

Chapter 2
"You'll Be Home in Three Days' Time. . ."

Of the four sons of the Tanner family, Ernie ("Ent") and Jakob ("Jack") were the two youngest. The Tanners resided in Winterthur, Switzerland. Father Tanner was a quiet, hardworking insurance agent. He, his wife Rosa, and the boys lived in a one-family row house. He had a big heart, often empathizing with the needs of fellow human beings. This virtue, however, created a lot of problems for his own family.

One man, a clerk who Ernie remembered as "Gisler," knew how to make himself at home. He pulled every string with Ernie's father, embellishing his problems. His father naively believed him. Month after month, then, he lived at the house, sucking large amounts of money out of the family. While Father Tanner was out working hard, Gisler sat in the kitchen stuffing his face. When little Ent gave him a funny look, Gisler threatened him with, "If you give me away, I'll break your face." This parasite was a miserable burden for the entire family. The children really suffered under his presence. The older brothers soon began to look for ways to strike out on their own. As Ent was finishing his schooling, his daydreams took him more and more frequently to distant shores.

In his spare time, Ernie secretly went looking for a job. He found one as a courier for an appliance store. For his fourteen years, he was still quite short. He would ride through town on an oversized clunky bike, delivering packages to customers. Some of the parcels were quite big. One day, a man demonstrating a new gadget in front of the store gave him a compliment.

"Well, young man, so young and already working so hard? You must have a lot of plans!"

Taken somewhat by surprise, Ernie blurted out his secret.

"I want to move to the French-speaking part of Switzerland and find a job there," he answered. "That's the reason I need money—to get there."

"I see!" the man replied. He thought for a moment, rubbing his chin a couple of times. He looked the boy over.

"Well," he said, "what do you want to do over there? Work in a hotel?"

A hotel? Ernie hardly knew anything about them. He had never been to one. His father did not think much of affiliating with the high-society clientele of such establishments. Sundays, for example, were not for gaffing at ladies in hats in hotels. They were for going to church, for a walk, for having a picnic. The most exciting thing they might do was visit grandmother during the school break. But visit a hotel? Never. And then opt to work in one?

"Why not?" Ernie responded quickly. "Yup, that's what I wanna do."

He rode back to the store on that large bike the following week. The salesman was there, too, and handed him a note. On it was written the address of a hotel. It was a day Ernie would never forget.

That note in his pocket was his ticket away from home. It would bring him closer to his goal: getting away from Gisler and his threats. There was also one other thing driving him away...that huge, gray building. Its entrance seemed to swallow up everyone who entered. He could see a staircase with people scurrying up and down it. There were too many offices to count, and they appeared to produce nothing more than papers with numbers. His father worked in that building of the insurance company. Ent had accompanied him there a few times. How he dreaded those drab walls! He even had an inkling that his father was planning for his youngest to follow in his footsteps. He reached into his pocket. Yes, the note was still there—like a key unlocking the whole wide world for him. On the way home, he began to daydream again.

The school year was slowly coming to an end. Spring flowers were blossoming all over Winterthur. One evening, the Tanner family was gathered in the living room. The brothers were excited about finishing the sixth grade, talking about their expectations for the future and career possibilities. Their father, though leaning over a book, was listening with one ear. Suddenly, he heard Ent's voice, "I'm going to go work in the French part of Switzerland."

"You wanna do what, boy?" his father said, interrupting their conversation. "Head over to the French part? Well, go ahead and do what you want, but you won't get a penny from me."

Undaunted, the boy laughed.

"Okay, Dad, I'll take you up on that. I'll go do whatever I want. After all, I already have the money for the trip together."

When his father learned that Ent already had the address of a hotel, his face became flushed. He didn't know whether to be mad or sad. Quickly, he regained his composure. As if to comfort himself, he told his son, "You'll find out soon enough what a hotel is. I'm sure you'll be back home in three days' time."

Those were words that Father Tanner should never have uttered! Over the next few years, Ernie would think about them over and over again. Every time he wanted to cry, every time his schoolboy French would fail him, every time his boss would yell at him, every time he would wash dishes at the sink way too high for him, every time he would drop into bed very late at night, he would remember those words. Then, he would grit his teeth and vow, "No, I won't give up at any price. There is no way I'll ever go back. Never!"

So he remained in the city of La Chaux-de-Fonds. At church, he enrolled himself in the confirmation course by his own choice. He patted himself on the shoulder, feeling very good about himself! He worked at the Fleur de Lys Hotel. Often, he managed to go to the movies in town, despite hard times. The war was on. Bread was being rationed. His boss needed it all for the hotel guests, not for his trainees. Oftentimes, Ernie would recall how Gisler used to snatch sandwiches away from him in the kitchen back home. Oh, how he coveted those sandwiches!

For three years in a row, Ernie was able to enjoy springtime in the Jura Mountains between France and Switzerland. He loved this season. He could hardly wait for a day off, particularly when he was sure the daffodils would be blooming. He would walk through the golden meadows, picking as many as he could possibly carry with both hands. Back home, he would fill every bottle and every jar he had with bunches of them. Then he would decorate his table, the windowsill, even the floor and the staircase leading up to his pitiful little room.

The time came for a certain season in his apprenticeship. These were years of traveling, training, and working in different hotels all over Switzerland. Some of them were large, well-known hotels; others were small and unassuming. No matter where he was, he would always take an interest in the people around him, whether co-workers, bosses or guests. He would observe them carefully to see their reactions in various situations. He would then put them into categories. Some were generous and friendly. Others were flatterers and hypocrites. Some were reserved while others were talkative. Still others were silly, and some, smart.

He took a temporary job at a hotel called the Schweizerhof in the city of Bern. There he visited an art exhibition. Tizian's paintings made quite an impression upon him. He set off to buy paint, brushes and canvas. He wanted to try taking up painting himself. That was another memorable day in his life. As far as the arts were concerned, Bern had a lot to offer. Hobby painters eager to learn more could take classes at the arts and trades school. That was just the thing for Ernie! Unfortunately, as his job at the Schweizerhof came to an end, his painting career did, too–for the time being.

Chapter 3
Fanny's Dream

It is the year 1955. We catch up with Ernie Tanner teaching at the Hotel Rosat Bible School in the city of Chateau d'Oex. Once a shy and introverted boy, he has been transformed into an exciting, enthusiastic teacher and speaker. He even conducts the school's choir. In his spare time, he ventures out into the streets and marketplaces, inviting many people to follow the Lord Jesus. He preaches in the surrounding villages. Sometimes he even picks up believers in a little van to take them to conferences in Chateau d'Oex. A young female teacher called Hedi attends one evening, listening intently. For a very brief moment, a thought takes form deep in her heart, "Wouldn't it be nice to be his wife?" If he only somehow knew....

His trips often brought Ernie into southern Germany, where he met many families with children. He had a particular weakness for the kids. Together with Fanny, a German employed by the Bible school, he decided to give organizing children's retreats a try. Soon, a once-in-a-lifetime opportunity arose in Bad Duerrheim in the Black Forest. An old health spa facility stood empty. It had not been used in ages and had only been occupied by the military temporarily. It was centrally located, which was ideal. It also had a delightful park nearby, long abandoned, where the kids could play.

Fanny received permission without any difficulty at all to hold the retreat there. The problems only started once they took a good look at the five-story building. They would have to fix toilets, repair old pipes, set up sleeping quarters, scrub floors and sweep out the rooms. A large stove had to be hoisted into the spacious, empty hotel kitchen. Tables and benches were brought into the large dining hall. Empty rooms were filled with straw for the kids to sleep on.

About forty children were expected to come, mostly from large, impoverished families. Fanny wanted to cook for the kids. The only thing missing was a volunteer to help care for the little tykes. Ernie thought a teacher would be the perfect person. The retreat would take place during summer break, anyway, which was a teacher's vacation time. He followed his instincts and turned out to be right. The teacher agreed to join the team. Zealously, they continued doing what needed to be done. In their old vehicle, a Borgward, the three of them drove everywhere, collecting food, such as potatoes, eggs, bacon, vegetables and so on. "Collecting" was just another way of saying "begging" for these things.

One morning, Ernie came over to pick up the two women at Fanny's apartment.

"Last night, I had a dream," Fanny said as he entered, "about you!"

"Well, isn't that something? We didn't get married, did we?"

"No! Sit down here, will you? It was exciting. You were sitting at a table, just like here! And you know what you were doing? Guess! You were counting money! Lots of money. It was no small change either! No, sir, you were counting out big bucks! You made lots of piles with those bills. That was the whole dream."

"Great!" said Ernie. "Where was I?"

"No idea," Fanny replied.

Whenever money got tight in the days that followed, Ernie would just laugh and say, "Tell me again where that dream took place?" If a farmer's wife did not have potatoes and gave them five Deutschmarks instead, he would grin and say, "Just like in the dream!" No one would ever have believed that twenty-five years later, Ernie would be counting out many, many bills to pay for a helicopter for his mission.

The day for the kids to arrive finally came. A welcome sign hung on the gate. Little flags were in the windows. Some dear ladies, faithful believers, were up early, ready to welcome the children. They looked forward to giving them some much-needed mothering. The musty rooms had taken on nearly a majestic atmosphere. The children laughed and made so much noise that no one really noticed anything missing.

One particularly mild evening, everybody gathered in the garden. As a surprise, "Uncle Ernie" was going to draw a picture with chalk right in front of their eyes. The audience was very attentive. Many people from the village, even the mayor, had come out to join them. Ernie kept everything quite mysterious. After a while, the onlookers could begin making out what was on the large illuminated canvas: high, rocky cliffs, and at the base, a little lamb. Large seagulls circled over the valley. The sky seemed to be getting darker and darker in the picture. Then, a surprise! In luminous colors, Ernie added the figure of a shepherd, reaching out to rescue the little lamb in danger.

Everyone had been watching carefully and admiring Ernie's artwork. Now that the picture was complete, many exclaimed, "Oh, how lovely!" But what was going on? The sky above them had gone dark, too! All at once, large drops of rain were splattering down all over the canvas. No one had seen the rain clouds approaching. One person after the other pulled his jacket over his head and ran off, seeking shelter. Only Ernie stayed behind. Quickly, he rolled up the electrical cord and hastily covered up the chalk he had been using. He then looked toward the house, in search of possible help. Yes, one other person had not gone. She was covering up some of the chalkboards with blankets. It was the teacher!

The heavy rain turned into hail. It hammered down with a loud, rushing sound. Quickly, Ernie picked up a chair and lifted it over his head to protect himself and the loyal teacher from the pellets. They were forced to stand close. He looked at her as the thunder and lightning resounded all around them. The two started laughing over the situation. Then he kissed her, still holding the chair over them with both hands. It was a good thing that the storm was so loud; at least he could not hear the wild beating of her heart.

"How wonderful!" she thought. "It's storming inside and out!"

The storm blew over just as quickly as it came. The volunteers ventured back outside to carry the wet utensils into the house. Ernie and Hedi looked at each other one more time. Their eyes revealed their thoughts, "It was meant to happen like that, and it was just fine that it did."

It was not the last retreat they would head up together. They put on many summer camps thereafter. There were always many reasons to jump for joy. Sometimes the duties included wiping away children's tears. Still, years later, they would receive the payoff. Often, they had the privilege of hearing, "We learned that lesson in one of your summer camps back then." Certainly, that is the kind of fruit that lasts, isn't it?

Hedi Dettweiler, the teacher from Dachsen at the Rhine River, returned home. So did Ernie Tanner. He went back home to his Bible school students in Chateau d'Oex. Soon, it became clear that this would not be home for good. He needed to move on...and he did. He found a new assignment waiting for him in Offenburg, Germany, where he was founder of a Christian fellowship church. From that base, he would go to minister in various small churches every week. These churches truly appreciated his joyful, edifying way of ministering. Of course, he did not forget about "his" teacher, even though he could only visit her occasionally.

About two years later, they had a big, happy wedding party in Aldingen, near Tuttlingen, in Germany. Guests came from all over. There was even a busload of students who came all the way from Switzerland.

"So, you want to be a preacher's wife?" the bride was asked by an older sister. "Do you have any idea of what you are getting into?"

"Well, I can imagine what it means," she answered, somewhat timidly.

"You'll have to manage being alone a lot. Will you be able to do that?" the sister wanted to know.

"I will, by the grace of God," she added thoughtfully. What a strange conversation! She would never forget it. The date was October 13, 1957.

Chapter 4
"How Much Does That Field Cost?"

Hedi and Ernie were living in a tiny apartment on the top floor of the building. His American friends called him "Ernie;" and, to his wife, the name perfectly suited the man she loved. They had a small living room with a coal oven for heat. In that room also stood a couch that could be converted into a bed, two armchairs you could hardly get by, and a small table. The bedroom had simply two beds and a wardrobe. The kitchen was right under the roof with diagonal walls going from the ceiling to the floor on both sides. The citizens of Dachsen were surprised about the developments in Hedi's life. They had been sure that their devout teacher was never going to get married. Well, she had proven them wrong!

After their first child was born, the young couple moved to the town of St. Georgen, Germany, in the Black Forest. Being a mother for the first time, Hedi was terribly worried that the move might be detrimental to her little boy. However, the landlady in the new place was very friendly. She offered help in both word and deed. She made it easier for Mrs. Tanner to get used to the new surroundings. Soon Hedi felt at home.

Working with children and teenagers was just as much on their hearts as at the beginning. They immediately began looking for a way of turning their retreats into somewhat more civilized events. This meant seeking out a more permanent setting for them. After many disappointments, they were finally able to buy a secluded farm on a mountainside. It had a magnificent view of a typical Black Forest valley. The woods, which started right behind the farmhouse, were wonderful and full of blueberries. The place seemed like a dream. Then came the rude awakening.

Ernie and many of the youth had gone to work building a new water supply system, including a reservoir, as well as an access road in the neighborhood. They worked themselves to the bone. Then, they received an unpleasant letter from the local agricultural department. The contract had been declared null and void, and they would reimburse them the purchase price. Ernie himself was not a farmer, which meant the contract did not comply with department regulations. Well, if that were not a big hint from God to return to Switzerland and start a youth ministry...

It was 1963. The Tanner family had grown to a household of five. They decided to move back to the Appenzellerland in Switzerland. There, they would live in a real, little Appenzeller house dating back a century or two. This is what Ernie Tanner wrote about it:

Both Hedi and I were convinced way deep down that we were to return to Switzerland. We decided to contact a real estate agency. The folks there managed to drum up a number of good offers. We looked at large and small houses all over the place—from the Jura Canton to the Bern Region, from the Seeland to the Zurich Upperland. They were either too expensive or too large, or the locations were not sunny enough. We couldn't make a decision and found ourselves, once again, back at the real estate agent's office in Zurich.

"Well, we still have a small house in the Appenzeller Canton in northeastern Switzerland!" the agent said, handing us another piece of paper.

I shook my head, remarking, "Moving to the Appenzellerland—to all those holiday resort charlatans. No way in the world!"

"But, Mr. Tanner," he replied, "there are also other people there, for example, the kids at the Pestalozzi Children's Village. Who knows, you just might like it there!"

"Hedi, what do you think? Should we have a look? Just to make sure it's not the right thing for us?"

"Well, it just might be worth taking a trip over there," my wife said with a big smile.

We were told that a Dutchman, a retired judge, was intending to sell his house in Trogen. His wife and he were growing older. It was getting harder for them to make their way down to the village. They had indicated wanting to sell to an artist or other idealistically-minded person.

The house had been built in the middle of a field and could only be reached by a narrow path. There we were! It was empty and spotlessly clean, made of solid wood. The walls were made of crossed beams. The doors to the different rooms were decorated with various antique metal fittings. We strolled from room to room, ducking our heads when entering a room. We ended up in the living room, which had an original Appenzeller stove bench behind the coal oven made of brown tiles. There were four sash windows toward the south. They overlooked a meadow, giving us a view of the north side of the mountain.

"Is this it, Lord?" I prayed silently. Then I turned to the Dutchman. "I think this is the right spot for us. Will you sell to us?"

In a nearby café, we sealed the deal. I have not regretted it since. We were able to take over the mortgage and pay what was still needed through savings. I considered it a true gift of God.

Of the eight rooms in the house, some were very small. They were not exactly suitable for summer camps for kids. Ernie, therefore, immediately started drawing up construction plans. Over the following five years, they became reality...bit by bit. Ernie prayed, planned some more, and went on building. One day, the neighbor across the road had a serious expression on his face. He was the one who kept selling him pieces of land every time expansion was needed. As he and Ernie met on the field, he mentioned this in passing.

"Well, Tanner, things are easy for you," he complained. "You just go pray and then get what you want. We others have to sweat bricks to get ours!"

He was not totally wrong, but Ernie, next to praying, did do his share of sweating as well.

One afternoon, he was sitting in his living room. Slowly, he fixed his gaze on the outdoor surroundings. He looked at the wooden fence, less than sixty feet from his house, which encompassed the lawn. Then he transferred his gaze to further down the road. While he was taking it all in, he also "took possession" of the land in his heart.

"Hedi, I think we should buy that piece of land behind the fence. It would make a great playground for the summer camp kids."

"Oh, that'd be nice, but what's it going to cost?" she answered. "You know, we have to consider that."

How typical! Money was never an issue for Ernie, but Hedi would start calculating right away. Ernie went over to have a talk with the neighbor. Soon, a land survey was done, and a price was agreed upon. When the bill came, Hedi threw her hands in the air.

"My goodness, we will never, ever be able to pay all of that! All those square feet. Let me see that. But this is for the entire area," she remarked, "not just the size of the field we want."

Ernie got hopping. "I'll check that out right away. Let me ring up the registry of deeds."

Still, he didn't worry about a thing. After making the call, he tried to calm his wife down. He told her that a letter confirming the proper size of the land would be coming within the next few days.

In the meantime, God had been doing some calculating Himself. Just one day later, Ernie received a letter from his older brother: their parents' house in Winterthur had been sold. The inheritance was to be split among the four brothers. Ernie's part would be 10,070 Swiss-Francs.

Shortly thereafter, the letter with the corrected number of square feet arrived. The price for the field came to 10,080 Francs.

"How do you like that, Hedi?" he said happily. "Don't we serve a loving God? Wouldn't you call this an act of provision in our time of need?"

Now even Hedi was astonished – and moved to tears of joy! She had to admit it was a truly wonderful God they were serving!

Ernie's evangelistic outreach events in Switzerland, Germany, Austria, Hungary and Yugoslavia were very blessed. He would invite all the children he met to come to Appenzell in the summertime. And come they did....

This meant more construction. First, a new access road to the house was needed. Then, Ernie stayed busy building new showers and new lavatories, a meeting room and a storeroom to serve all those children. When more rooms became necessary later on, he built another story on top of them.

Then the time came for a new foundation to be laid.

"Today," he said one day, "the concrete will be delivered! Let's get to work."

Some friends plus Hedi, Maria and Carmen stood ready to go. Sure enough, a large truck drove up and dumped the first load on the site.

"At what time will you need the next load?" the driver asked.

No one had any clue as to how long it would take to use up the first batch of concrete. After a moment's thought, Ernie made a hasty decision, confidently saying, "At 11 o'clock." He was convinced they would be ready by then. Now, everyone was shoveling like mad. One wheelbarrow after another was being filled up. Then, they had to stamp down the concrete. After a short break, they went at it again.

Suddenly, someone called out, "The concrete is coming!"

He was right. The truck was coming back with the second load. They had just finished using the first one! They continued shoveling diligently, albeit somewhat slower, taking more breaks. They showed each other the blisters and calluses they had "earned." One complained about his back; another, about his feet. The women's arms were getting heavier and heavier. Nevertheless, everybody was laughing and working joyfully.

A bit later, someone else yelled, "There's more concrete coming!"

Where? All heads turned. Someone was just pulling their leg.

Then, once again, the warning sounded, "The concrete is coming!"

Already? But they hadn't finished up the last load yet. Now they really had to hurry up. Before evening, another load was to be delivered. Everything had to be used up that day.

"The concrete is coming! The concrete is coming!"

The children were shouting it to cheer on the workers. Everyone was shoveling with all his might. Whenever Maria would stop to lean on her shovel and catch her breath, Carmen would tease her, "The concrete is coming."

Before suppertime, the three volunteers left. Hedi put the children to bed. At the end of the day, one small heap of concrete was left over. Using their last bit of strength, Ernie and the women poured it into the foundation. Then, they washed up their tools, packed them up and, finally, sat down, exhausted, on the bench in front of the house. It had gotten dark.

"And now, my dears," the ever-energetic Ernie announced, "we are headed 'for the stars' where we'll be served the meal of a lifetime. We deserve it!"

That dinner at a special restaurant turned out to be a real treat after a hard day's work.

Chapter 5

The Beginning of All Wisdom

In the years since they had gotten married, Hedi had had the chance to put one good virtue into practice: patience. If Ernie had promised to return home on a Thursday, she would look out the window early in the morning.

"Is that his car I hear driving in? No," she would tell herself, "that's impossible. He couldn't be back this early."

Then, while braiding the girls' hair, she would remind them that Daddy would be coming home that day.

"Will he be home for lunch?" Immanuel, the oldest son, wanted to know. He could already tell time.

The time of waiting was filled with happy anticipation. At lunchtime, however, one seat still remained empty.

"He must have met someone to tell about Jesus!" the boy tried to appease himself. "He'll surely come while we're taking our nap. Then, all of a sudden, he'll just be there!"

After naptime, one still sleepy-eyed yet curious face after the other reappeared.

"Is he back yet?"

"No, not yet. There must be a lot of traffic. He'll be home soon."

Again Hedi looked down the street. As the time passed, the waiting became more tedious. By now, she was struggling with worry.

"Something just might have...no!" she scolded herself, determining to reject those fearful thoughts.

She busied herself with knitting while the children played. Suppertime was over, but Ernie had still not arrived. The children headed for bed and remembered to include their daddy in their prayers. Mom sat at the window. Finally, she spotted his headlights as the car drove up. Ernie entered, lovingly taking his wife into his arms.

"Got a lot of knitting done today, did you?" he asked smilingly. "Well, I've brought you a few nice things."

Then they emptied out the trunk together. There were apples, eggs, flowers and homemade bread. The children stood at the door, wide-eyed.

"Daddy is like Santa Claus," one boy observed. "First you have to wait a long time for him to come, but when he does, he brings lots of goodies."

When the kids were back in bed, Ernie explained to his wife why he had arrived later than expected. He had picked up some hitchhikers, as he often did. The three young men had no choice but to sit in the backseat: all of his maps, letters and his breakfast were strewn across the passenger seat. They were students who wanted to spend their vacation in Switzerland.

"Well, we have some time for a conversation," he thought. Looking into the rearview mirror, he opened up with, "So, you all are going to university? That's where you get real smart, right? Then I'm sure you'll be able to answer this one question, 'What is the beginning of wisdom?'"

He was careful to speak very slowly, giving them time to think about it. Silence, at first. Then, the sound of throats being cleared.

"That's a tough one," they answered. "Let's see. The beginning...."

Ernie decided to help them out.

"The Bible says, 'The fear of the LORD is the beginning of wisdom' (Proverbs 9:10). Let me show you how I can prove it. What are you studying?"

"Medicine."

"Law."

"Theology."

Ernie deliberated briefly. This certainly wasn't going to be easy, but he sensed God wanted to talk to these young men.

"You are majoring in medicine, right?"

He continued driving as if on cruise control while addressing the first one.

"Well, God says in His Word that He is the Lord, our Doctor. If you allow this Doctor to rule in your life and receive Him into your heart, then—and only then—can you become a truly excellent doctor."

He looked at the one sitting in the middle through his mirror.

"You are a law student, aren't you?" he confirmed. "King Solomon went down in history as the wisest judge ever, and he was quoted as saying, 'A divine sentence is in the lips of the king: his mouth transgresseth not in judgment' (Proverbs 16:10). Do you see how smart it is to read the Bible?"

"And you are studying theology?" he asked the third young man.

"Yeah, but this is only my first year," he admitted. Apparently, he had no intention whatsoever of being dragged into a theological argument. That wasn't what Ernie had in mind either.

"Have you ever given your life to Christ...been converted, that is?" he asked casually.

After thinking a brief moment, he answered rather unconvincingly, "Well, in fact, yeah, I have. But I'm not into tooting my horn about it."

"What was the basis for all of St. Paul's messages?" Ernie asked, immediately giving the answer. "Was it not the testimony of his conversion? This testimony should be the foundation and jumping-off point for every theologian. Make sure that before you step behind any pulpit, you have had a personal experience with God. You will be responsible for the souls of a church. How do you intend to lead people if you yourself are not led by God?"

It got very quiet in the car. They were close to the city of Schaffhausen, their destination. Ernie slowed down and stopped the car at the side of the road.

"If you don't mind, I'd like to pray for you guys."

They agreed. Saying good-bye, they thanked him warmly and went merrily on their way.

Chapter 6
New Territory

Letters from Africa! They had come in from all over: Cameroon, Congo-Brazzaville, Kenya and Uganda. The writers shared fascinating stories about their missionary work. Some also wrote of natives who were evangelizing their own villages. Still others wrote more directly, "Come over and help us." The white envelopes simply lay on his desk, but Ernie Tanner heard them talking to him every single day. Whether working or praying, he would see those letters before him. He wondered over and over again whether it could be God's will for him to travel to Africa.

He hesitated making plans until the fall of 1968. He asked himself, first of all, if it were wise to spend all that money on a plane ticket. Besides, there was a lot of work waiting for him at home in Switzerland. A letter from his cousin Otto, a missionary in Cameroon, played the decisive role. Otto asked Ernie to come hold evangelistic services in his churches.

All of the packing and preparations for Ernie's first trip brought a lot of excitement into their lives—and a lot of questions. In early 1969, it was time for the Tanner family to board a train for Zurich. On the way, there were still lots of things to clarify. Ernie admonished all the children one more time to be obedient and to help their mother. A Swissair shuttle bus then took them to the airport.

The five of them, that is, Hedi, Immanuel, Miriam, Damaris, and little Simon who had just turned four, stood at the railing of the open terrace. The parting was somewhat painful for everyone. Anxiously, they looked over to the area where their daddy would soon be boarding the airplane. He turned around and waved with his handkerchief. He got on board with the other passengers, disappearing from sight.

Hedi and the children stayed for the departure. Slowly, the plane rolled to a stop at its take-off position on the runway. The engines blared, going full speed and propelling the machine forward. Then, it was airborne.

Suddenly a loud protest cut through the air, "Daddy's going to heaven. Simon wanna go to heaven, too!"

The little guy stretched out his hands, crying and in great distress. His mother took him in her arms and held him tight. She could not utter a word herself. Then, the three other kids started crying as well. Hedi took all of them, as best she could, by the hand. She left the terrace as quickly as possible to evade the inquisitive looks of bystanders. At the train station kiosk, she bought five sandwiches, five eggs, five pastries, five apples and five pieces of chewing gum. Once they were on the train again, the kids forgot their agony. They chomped on the food and marveled at the world outside whizzing past them. One thing was for sure: it would be quite some time before Hedi would say farewell at an airport again. Saying good-bye at home was much easier.

Even though Ernie and Hedi's ways parted physically for a time that day at Kloten Airport, the two were still joined together in heart. They promised each other, "We shall meet again every morning at the throne of God!"

The Black Continent would leave an indelible impression upon Ernie. In a book in which he described receiving his call to Africa, he shared several of his initial experiences there. To him, they were like guideposts marking the way for the path he should take for the rest of his life. He wrote of having fellowship with missionaries and meeting indigenous pastors. He marveled at the women who carried their shopping goods on their heads. He studied the faces of the natives as they listened to him preach. He described encounters with wild animals and flying vermin. He felt compassion for the Africans as he flew over innumerable thatched huts and small villages. Driving a jeep over potholes was also part of the adventure. Whatever he was doing, a strong desire

to aid the people of Africa accompanied him. He began
to grasp that what they needed more than anything else
was to hear of God's love and to receive salvation through
His Son, Jesus Christ.

Ernie recounts a moving episode:

> One afternoon, we can hear people crying
> out loud. Obviously, some awful event has taken
> place. About thirty feet away from our quarters, a
> bush house is going up in flames. I put my slippers
> on and run over to the scene, camera in hand. I
> soon lose any interest in taking snapshots. The
> wooden house is ablaze with flames shooting out of
> the roof. In great desperation, the poor inhabitants
> begin grabbing what belongings they owned.
> While the roof is nearly consumed by the flames,
> I start helping them rescue what can be rescued.
> There is much shouting. The natives start vacating
> the house next door, barely six feet away. Its fate
> seems to be sealed!
>
> Suddenly, it occurs to me what needs to be
> done. I grab one bucket after the other and place
> them into the hands of the men who aren't thinking
> straight. They remain standing around helpless
> because, around here, men do not carry anything,
> including water—not even when there is a fire.
> Bound and determined, I grab the next bucket and
> run down to the riverbank. That says more than a
> thousand words. A white man is fetching water—
> and for the natives, at that!
>
> Everyone goes into action. Out of breath and
> soaking with sweat, I come back with water and
> pour it over the edge of the roof from the house next
> door. People yell as I must get close to the source
> of the fire. Others begin following my example.
> The water makes a hissing sound as it trickles
> down the sides of the walls. The house is saved!

The natives stand utterly amazed. Everywhere, I hear, "God bless you!"

The poor woman whose house was burned down is crying, shouting and jumping up and down–doing a type of dance–out of sheer desperation. It fills me with great sadness. I give her a few dollars for a new house and try to comfort her. Gratefully, she squeezes my hands, receiving the consolation.

Now, it is time to get to the street evangelization quickly. My face is as red as a tomato. On the way, I am introduced to the chief of the tribe. I recognize him as one of those I chased off to carry water. Politely, he expresses his gratitude and joins us for the street meeting. Many people begin gathering.

An African gets up on a table and begins to speak. I ask some people to help turn the table upside down and put it on top of a Volkswagen. I climb up there. Those standing around start cheering. To them, it is quite a spectacle. The interpreter also finds a place to stand up on my "pulpit." Now, things really get rolling. Through God's grace, the people seem to be opening up to the penetrating message. During prayer, a hush comes over the crowd. God is at work. We praise Him for this and invite everyone to come to church with us.

The most memorable experience of the trip occurred on the night before Ernie had to fly back. In Africa, they have what are called bush taxi cabs. The driver simply waits until his vehicle is full of passengers headed for the same destination. Only then does he put the vehicle into drive. Ernie had taken a seat in a seven-seater Peugeot van, just like the one he had at home. He was sitting in the center row next to an Indian and an African. In the back seat was an Indian couple. The driver and the daughter of the Indian sat in front. The van was not

able to go faster than fifty miles per hour, which turned
out to be an advantage. Thanks to that–and the grace of
God–they arrived in Nairobi without harm.

A couple of times, they saw elephants near the road.
Ernie asked the driver to stop the next time they did so
he could take a picture. The driver obliged him when one
appeared. Ernie got out of the car. He took a few steps
toward the elephant, speaking quietly and gently.

"Come on, Bobby, hold up for a minute. Let me have
a good look at you. My, aren't you something? Now, be a
good boy, Bobby."

Slowly, the elephant started shaking his head and
waving his large ears. Things were getting precarious!
"Bobby" was now raising up one leg. Ernie instantly took
a photo and jumped back into the car.

The distraction was short, though, and the ride
seemed to take forever. The passengers were cramped
together, and the roads were terrible. The men started
talking about politics. Often, to Ernie's dismay, the driver
would actually turn around to look at them while driving.
Everyone was talking loudly. All at once, they found
themselves driving in a ditch by the roadside. Pebbles
and sand were strewn all over. It took all of Ernie's self-
control to stay calm. Finally, the ride had come to an
end. Exhausted but relieved, he got out. He discovered
that his acquaintances were not home yet, and their door
was locked.

Evening had come. Ernie spread out on the lawn to
stretch his tired legs a bit. While looking up at the sky,
an overwhelming gratitude toward the Creator of all of
the stars flooded over him. Through his relationship to
Christ, the Creator had become his Father. He recalled
many encounters he had had in life–both good and bad,
past and future. There were opportunities he had taken
and ones he had missed.

Then, the black faces of Africa began looming before
him. It seemed as though he could tell what they were
thinking. He sensed what they were feeling, what

their deepest longings were, and how much they were suffering. What miserable darkness they were living in! The Africans were surrounded by ominous idols and oppressing spirits. So many of them had no concept of a loving Creator of that glorious, starry sky. Numbers of people were passing in front of Ernie's inner eye. He tried, with his actual eyes, to take in the vast panorama of the starry sky over Africa. As he did, a hitherto unfamiliar urge engulfed his soul: a great love for the African people. This love was strong enough to overcome any and all burdensome, bureaucratic intricacies necessary to reach them. This love would carry him through all kinds of disappointments, difficulties and demonic devices. It was the kind of love that God alone could give.

This experience at the end of his first visit to the continent would seal Ernie's future path. It was a source of strength from which he could draw at any point in time. It was an encouragement whenever doubts would assail him. God had revealed the soul of Africa to him; but, more than that, He had given him a burden he would never be able to shake off.

Chapter 7
"Expedition Gorilla Path"

"Taking everything into consideration," Ernie Tanner was explaining, pointing with a pencil, "I believe the best plan would be to march from here to there."

A map of Cameroon was spread out across the living room table of the Tanner's home in Trogen. He was indicating the very heart of the jungle. His wife and four children, along with co-worker Marcel Gasser, were pressing in close, eager to see.

Immanuel leaned over the table, spelling out, "Y-o-k-a-d-u-m-a. You want to start there and hike through this unknown territory all the way up to this village?! This is where Lomie is," he said with a slight groan. His index finger landed near Dad's pencil tip. You would have thought the ten-year-old would have to get up and walk through the jungle himself!

"But *why* do you have to go there, Daddy?" Immanuel's younger sister wanted to know.

Now, *that* would be very long story. During his first trip to Africa, Ernie had visited a former fellow-student. The man was now working as a missionary among the Pygmies in Congo-Brazzaville. It had been a very precious visit. First of all, the two were happy to be reunited again. Then, Ernie also had the chance to meet the Pygmies for the first time.

The Pygmies are notably short in stature. He remembered Joe Ellis telling him that years ago when he had first arrived at the Oubangui River. Back then, Joe had lived in a tent on its banks. He had slowly initiated a relationship with the bushmen. Since then, he had been able to win over a small crowd of Pygmies who enjoyed having fellowship with him. Ernie could only marvel at this.

Only very recently had the government recognized the Pygmies as human beings with the rights of citizens, he had learned. Prior to that, these natives, who made their living hunting and fishing, had been regarded as animals. Ernie had only been with them for a few days. He watched them carry out their competitions in canoeing and crossbow shooting. He looked on as they built "kitchens." He attended their open-air services. Ernie soon came to know and love these people, who only came up to his shoulder.

This people group lived hidden in the woods of the northern part of Congo and in the southern swamps of the Cameroonian jungle. It was this very area Ernie was focusing on now. It was an unknown spot on the map of Cameroon. There, he wanted to look for Pygmies and bring them the Good News. In Yaounde, the capital city, he had visited a theological institute to obtain information about these unusual tribesmen. He had tried to find out exactly where in the country they were living, but no one had been able to give him a clue. Out of experience, he knew the best thing would be to go there and check things out himself. He had made preparations, along with Marcel. They had bought all the necessities for surviving in the jungle. Now Ernie was deciding which route they should take. They would take care of the details once they arrived.

In just a couple of sentences, he answered the anxious question of his little daughter. It was very quiet in the living room. Many thoughts and questions, hopes and fears were racing through the minds of those present. Finally, Ernie, in his deep, calm voice, began praying. He asked his Father in heaven to grant wisdom and protection for this dangerous journey.

This time Hedi and Ernie's last embrace took place at home. Ernie and Marcel stepped into the fully-loaded car as Hedi and the kids waved good-bye. The driver blew the horn a couple of times as he slowly drove out of sight. Hedi went back into the house to put away everything left lying around from packing. Life at home went on. Meanwhile, a new chapter in the Africa story was opening up for the two pioneers.

In the car, hardly a word was spoken. Both Ernie and Marcel were wracking their brains to see if they had forgotten anything. Passport, visa, money? Ernie put his hand in his pocket. Everything was right there. In addition to their two suitcases, they were transporting a tent, sleeping bags, a tape recorder, a camera with film case, groceries, flares, tools, gifts for the natives, a compass and matches. They also had a firearm tucked away securely at the bottom of things. This was to defend themselves against wild animals.

The flight aboard a Swissair machine to Douala was uneventful. Thereafter, things started getting interesting and quickly ran off schedule! The wagon of the train they were riding in was overcrowded. Then, a truck took them by way of roads that didn't deserve the name. At last, they arrived in Yokuduma. They could finally get out and stretch their legs. The next item would be to look for a place to stay. The great challenge for the following day was finding Africans willing to serve as carriers for the long march. Ernie met some men, negotiated with them, and made out a written contract. At the same time, he became aware of a path already in existence which, though rarely used, led to Lomie. The natives respectfully called it the "Gorilla Path."

The day to "break camp" had come. The luggage was ready and waiting in front of the house where they had had to wait for a permit. That had taken a couple of days. Each of the carriers then received his piece of luggage. François took the suitcase, and Laurent, the military backpack. Jacques had the water and the backpack; Henri, the tent; Jean-Jacques, the guitar and the tent poles. Pascal took the groceries and the camera case. All of these things landed on the curly heads of the carrier team. Slowly, the caravan started out, led by Ernie Tanner, who carried his camera on one shoulder and the tape recorder on the other. On his belt, he had a small water bottle. He had a bush knife in one hand and a spear in the other. Marcel, carrying the video camera, formed the rearguard.

Other villagers lined the road, watching in astonishment. The morning dew drizzled down from the jungle trees onto the group as they entered into the green tunnel of the bush. The morning shower was pleasant, but the burning heat of the sun would soon dry it all up. Snakes and other creeping things fled at the constant, pounding sound of feet, shoes, boots, sandals. The sound of birds squawking nearby shattered the stillness. Words were spoken very rarely.

Everyone tried to adapt to the pace of the man in front of him – to keep up, fit in and become part of this small group. It was not a military line; the path wasn't made for this. At the onset, the path was a regular one in the woods, lined by low bushes, with bush trees forming a canopy above. After every hour they would take a five- to ten-minute break to drink some water. Then, they would exchange loads and march on, mile after mile. Each morning before they departed, they would filter water and take it with them.

If they reached some houses, a village or a clearing toward evening, they would stay there for the night. The first village they encountered was Mbol. The children stood in the doorways of their houses, staring at the strangers. The first order of the evening was always finding the head of each village. Sometimes the chief would look at the new arrivals with skepticism. Sometimes he looked rather aggravated! Then Ernie would quickly get out his Polaroid camera and make signs that he wanted to snap a photo. He would try speaking in French or ask the interpreter to explain why they had come. As soon as a chief would see his photo, his antagonistic expression would usually vanish, giving way to a grin. Ernie had been looking forward to the demonstration: he had bought the camera for this very purpose. The photo would then be his gift, sealing the brief friendship between the chief and himself.

Night after night, they would meet with the villagers and their respective leaders in the chief's hut. They would tell everyone, whether young or old, about God's unending love. There was such a great thirst in the Africans to know more about it. In the morning, they would leave behind new friends, often receiving a touching sendoff. The journey would continue. After a while, the path became nearly impassable. Often gigantic, fallen trees would block their passage. Every time, it took extra strength to climb over these enormous obstacles with their heavy loads. They also had to cross many rivers, some narrow and some wide. As a precautionary measure, they had brought air mattresses along. Each time, however, they would find a canoe tied up, available for crossing. This was helpful in not losing any precious time in blowing up the makeshift barges.

One day, half-an-hour after having passed through a village, the group heard yelling behind them. Three women were waving and shouting, trying to get their attention. At first, Ernie did not take notice. They were persistent in calling, however, and kept closing the gap between them. Ernie then asked everyone to stop. He asked his interpreter what they were saying.

"They want to talk to the white man," he answered.

Marcel and Ernie looked at each other. They did not really want to break their pace now. The march was strenuous enough. What problems were headed their way? Nonetheless, they waited for the women to catch up. They were wheezing, out of breath and sweating up a storm; still, you could see an excited determination in their eyes. The carriers put down their loads. Nearby was a clearing. A tree was lying across the path, making it the right place for a conversation. Ernie's interpreter communicated the request of these women.

A long time ago a man had come to visit them, one woman began. He had told them about a God who had come down to earth to help mankind because He loved them. He, however, had been killed. Everything went silent. What exactly did these women want from "the white man?"

"The man told us that this God would come back again," the second woman proceeded, "and would gather all those who believe in Him to Himself."

"Surely, the white man must know whether He has already come," a third woman concluded, gesturing toward Ernie.

All three stared at Ernie in anticipation. They were sitting together on the trunk of the tree. Once again, there was silence. Ernie was deeply moved. He had to search for the right words. Could something like this even be happening? Only once had these women heard about Jesus: now they were waiting impatiently for His return? Nothing could have given him greater pleasure than breaking the bread of life for these three hungry hearts. After a time of fellowship, the women allowed the group to proceed–with great reluctance. Their faces were radiant as they said good-bye.

Now and then, the men would find Pygmy huts close to the path. These were different from the other huts in every respect. They looked like small heaps of leaves and were so low that one could only sit or lie down in them. The people themselves were nowhere to be seen. Pygmies are known to be very afraid of other people. Sometimes they would appear in the villages, but would stand off by themselves.

Only once, on the fourth night of the journey, the team heard them dancing and making a type of noise... you really couldn't call it singing, as such. It turned out to be an ancient, traditional welcome. It deeply impressed the two Europeans. In return, they picked up their guitar and sang a song for the bush people. Then, they let them know why they had come, speaking through an interpreter. The Africans listened with open, willing hearts. The message had to be truly important if these white men had come from so far away to share it!

This time, the departure was different from others. The chief introduced them to a man with a rifle.

"He'll be accompanying you," the interpreter explained. "He can show you the way and help protect you on the next section of the path. It's particularly dangerous."

Ernie agreed to employ him as a guide and carrier–although he was not totally convinced of the reliability of the old firearm. The new man managed to fit into the group quickly. His local knowledge was a great asset.

The Gorilla Path was getting narrower all the time. Ernie had to start using his bush knife. The perseverance of the carriers was being sorely tested. Every day, it would take longer to reach the next destination. Hourly breaks had to be prolonged. The heat was taxing. The heavy loads and long distances were wearing them out. Once a shrieking horde of baboons scared them to bits. Another time they had to flee from a colony of army ants. At the sight of fresh elephant tracks, they got particularly nervous.

The man with the rifle always walked right behind Ernie. One day, he found something alarming by the side of the path. He pointed toward a thick pole rammed into the ground next to the path. It had a withered tuft of grass at the top.

"A bush man who used this path before us came across a predator right here. As a warning, he stuck this pole into the ground!"

The rifleman's supposition would be confirmed. Just about one hundred feet further, a second warning sign was set up as well.

"Here," he said nervously, "is the place where the big cat was. Another hundred feet away is the third warning for bushmen coming from the opposite direction."

The entire group continued on at a faster pace.

For Ernie, the moment also was enlightening. He came to see firsthand what stress and strain ministers take upon themselves to reach remote places. If they, although filled up with God's Spirit and Word, arrive totally exhausted or even sick at their destination, how can they minister to others? And how much valuable time is lost, not even considering the loss of energy!

"Isn't there any way to make the work of the missionaries, so eager to help, easier?"

That was Ernie's thought as he fought his way through the jungle, step by step. He would gaze at the bare tree trunks and let his eyes wander up to their tops. Then he would look up at the sky over them. Up there... way up above and beyond this lamentable path of roots and rocks and every imaginable obstacle, not to mention, the dangers...up there, it would be so much easier. You could fly, just keep moving forward...

Before reaching their destination of Lomie, they took one final break. Within seven days, they had trekked ninety miles through the jungle. They had reached the very limit of what their bodies could cope with. They had preached the Gospel in remote villages and huts. They had also gained detailed insight for developing an effective missions strategy. Ernie's understanding and appreciation for missionaries had certainly grown! Even more than that, he had been inspired–inspired to set a high goal for himself: he wanted to provide help for pioneers on the mission field.

The group had grown into a unit in the short period of time. They came together for a final meeting. They received their promised wages, plus a good tip as well. How their black faces beamed! When it was finally time to say farewell, their eyes grew misty. The hearts of the natives were also not without fear. The dark jungle path leading back to their village lay ahead of those brave "burden-bearers." They had grown to appreciate Ernie. Although he had often been a tough leader, he had motivated them to perform in a manner far surpassing the usual African way of thinking. Now they had to head back. They kept waving and waving and waving until the jungle, so familiar and yet so harrowing, swallowed them up again.

Chapter 8
Otto's Old "Toy"

A very important chapter had come to a close for
Ernie and Marcel—but the story was really just beginning.
The second phase of their Africa trip was still ahead of
them. In Lomie, they found a truck to take them back to
civilization. They visited Ernie's cousin Otto, who headed
up a large mission in Kumba. With him, they planned
to have a look at Ngwandi, a large and very remote
mountain village. Even though this mission would only
take two days, a whole troop of carriers would be needed
to transport everything.

The settlement consisted of various villages, all
situated on a flat mountain ridge. It was nicely built,
and each village had its own large square. This was
ideal for open-air gatherings. Ample opportunities to
hold them presented themselves, and the listeners were
always extremely attentive. Many Africans would open
their hearts to God's wooing and submit their lives to
the Lord Jesus. At the end of the meeting, everyone
would join together in singing joyful songs; they could
be heard for miles. Afterward, when tracts were being
distributed, it would cause such a ruckus that the poor
guy handing them out was followed by a swirling cloud of
dust everywhere he went!

Once again, the time to say good-bye was drawing
closer. In every place he went, Ernie would leave a part
of his heart behind. In return, he would take a sackful
of wonderful memories back with him. The strong,
clear voices of the women from Ngwandi, for example,
continued ringing in his heart for a long time. Despite the
heavy loads they toted around on their heads, they were
always singing. One favorite tune was, "We are walking
in the light...we are walking in the light of God." These
robust, barefooted women were used to rugged mountain
trails. They offered to Ernie to carry the luggage half

the way and then to return to their village. In the end, they accompanied the evangelists for the entire six hours to their starting point where the Volkswagen van was waiting.

Otto, Ernie, Marcel and the interpreter used boats and buses to get from place to place. Often, going on foot was the only option. Almost everywhere they went, they were received with joy. Tired and sweaty, they would come back to Otto's house at night. Otto's wife Waltraud could never tell what made Ernie happier–the primitive shower at the back of their house or the blue airmail letter from Switzerland. Ernie relished both thoroughly.

"How are things going at home?" Waltraud inquired.

"Oh, everything's fine...well, apart from a couple of minor things. Simon ran around, stumbled and hit a wall with his little head. The doctor had to stitch it up. Hedi says it's healing well. We'll hardly be able to see the scar by the time he's grown," Ernie comforted himself.

"What about the girls?" she wanted to know.

"Well, I miss my little girl, the way she laughs. Miriam had a fever and had to stay in bed. Hedi had to do leg compresses and spent the night at her bedside." He paused, contemplating a moment. "I'll be very glad to get back home!"

"How does Hedi cope with being by herself for so long? Isn't she afraid of being alone in such a big house?"

"She didn't write anything of that nature. She's a brave woman, you know. I am so proud of her. I'm convinced that she understands my ministry and supports everything I do. She's my best cheerleader. If that weren't the case, I wouldn't be able to leave home all the time. There will always be 'hellos' and 'goodbyes', times of separation and times of fellowship. She knows that. You know, Waltraud,..." he confided, seeming to ponder something over, "...letters are nice, but they also make you yearn all the more to get back. Just a couple more days!"

Something was going on outside of the window, which was only covered with a thin wire grate. Rustling, huffing and puffing, giggling. Then, the heads of some kids popped up. Big, curious eyes peeped through the lattice to find out what the white men were doing.

"What kind of bad fashion this be for looking so inside we room?!" Otto yelled, clapping his hands. The heads disappeared. They did not need an interpreter to understand his Pidgin English.

Otto had, for years, been the overseer of many churches with indigenous preachers. He had gained plenty of experience in dealing with young and old.

"It's not that easy being a missionary nowadays. There is a strong sense of national identity in the African nations freed from colonialism," he explained. "Whites are no longer as well-respected as before. They are tolerated as long as they bring social, financial or spiritual help. We have to be very wise and make sure to remain in the background. We must teach and train the Africans, and then let them take the lead. They need us, but we mustn't rub it in. They are like our grown-up children," Otto said, starting to laugh. Then, he patted his old Bible.

"What we need to give them is a good 'toy' to play with."

He was persuaded that a living, practical form of Christianity would help Africans in every area of their lives—and not just them either.

Otto wrote to friends of the Tanner family:

Kumba
March 18, 1970

Dear Friends,
    At the beginning of the year, we had the pleasure once again of welcoming Ernie Tanner and his fellow-laborer, Marcel Gasser, to the mission field. We had prepared a very full itinerary

well in advance, which kept them busy for three full weeks.

After a very encouraging ten-day mission in the coastal area, I had the honor of accompanying Ernie into the grassland. For me, those next ten days were an especially blessed and refreshing time of fellowship. Market squares and roadside meadows served as open-air venues for the evening crusades. After finding the right spot, we would set up our speakers; it took no time at all. Drawn by the music, people would form a circle around us, getting in close to hear. We were then able to share a clear, life-bringing Gospel message with them.

I remember two nights in particular. We had reserved them for a larger village. A big crowd of people of all ages gathered around us. It looked very promising. They enjoyed listening to our songs. Then, in reverential silence, they paid close attention to the simple, appealing message. Visibly moved, many responded to the call to follow Christ. The Spirit of God was surely moving. We invited them to join us in singing a chorus. This they did joyfully and voluntarily, which is rather unusual, even for Africans. To us, it was proof of God's working among them: that is the only explanation for it. Before you knew it, a French chorus was resounding throughout the area. The words in English went, "I am happy, for Jesus has saved me. In love He forgave me. Therefore, I sing that I am happy, for Jesus has saved me."

Since that mission, we have been able to hold meetings there regularly. For me, it was like being in our home church. It didn't feel like an open-air crusade at all because, up until then, I'd never seen people singing along so spontaneously. At the close, we had reached the "critical" phase, distributing the tracts everyone wanted. Experience taught us to put all the equipment back into our car first. Then, we handed a bunch of tracts to each of the especially strong men whom we had instructed beforehand. They had to press their way into the crowd as far as they could before starting to give them out. They did not make it very far, though, before the fighting started. We just barely managed to escape it. The only solution was getting into the car. We had no other choice but to sneak away from the begging crowd pushing in around us.

It hurt to see that we only had a limited number of tracts for so many hungry souls. We are all the more grateful for those 10,000 tracts and the 60,000 copies of the Gospel of John which Ernie sent us a couple of weeks ago. We would like to take this opportunity to thank all of you, our friends, very much. It was you who made this possible through your sacrificial giving. May God reward you richly!

Greeting you warmly in the love of Jesus,

Otto and Waltraud Tanner

Part Two

Chapter 9
"You've Got to be Kidding!"

Ernie flew home, his spirit filled with impressions of the past three months. He couldn't keep his thoughts from racing ahead. He began making plans for the not-too-distant future. Something was about to happen–of that he was certain. He could feel something being stirred up inside of him.

A tumultuous welcome from his loved ones awaited Ernie. He was grateful to see them again–all safe and sound–and locked each one in his arms for a long hug. Then, it was time to talk. And talk. And talk. Every one of the children had something very important to tell Daddy which he simply "had to know." He inspected Simon's eyebrow, which the doctor had stitched up so well. Finally, it was their father's turn to tell some stories. His listeners were all ears....

"...so, I am telling you, kids, those tribes cut off from civilization are really open to the Gospel. We must pray for God to show us a way to reach those Africans much faster," Ernie concluded seriously. The kids were speechless, for a change. So much had been said. They all folded their hands and prayed for the next step.

The summer and the annual retreats brought much work. Ernie also held evangelization crusades in different places in Switzerland. Together with Marcel, he traveled on to Hungary and Yugoslavia. Wherever he went, he challenged his listeners to make a commitment to God. Whether hiking mountains with the kids during summer camp or taking part in a prayer meeting or just sitting behind the steering wheel, Ernie could not shake Africa. It just wouldn't leave him alone.

One day, he was especially upset when he came home.

"Did you hear the news on the radio?" he asked his wife. "Another six US army helicopters have been shot

down in Vietnam, directly over the jungle. All hope of
rescue seems lost. But the army is simply sending in
new machines. They must have a whole bunch of them.
You can't top those whirlybirds. They can take off from
anywhere!" Ernie was bubbling over.

"We should have one for the mission. What do you
think about that, Hedi, dear?"

He didn't wait for a reply. Nor did he take any
interest in lunch or the mail that day. All he could see
before his eyes were helicopters cruising over treetops in
the jungle.

"I should learn how to fly!" The thought occurred to
him, but he almost didn't dare to speak it out. Then, he
inquired, "Hedi, what would you say if I learned to fly?"

"Are you crazy, my dear?" Hedi laughed. "You've got
to be kidding...or have you struck it rich?"

"Yeah, yeah, I'm joking," Ernie seemingly closed
the conversation. He got up and disappeared into the
bedroom.

The following Sunday afternoon, he asked his family
to get into the car.

"Let's get outta here before any more visitors show
up!"

"But where are we going?"

"You'll see soon."

"To the lake!" guessed one child.

"No, to the *Steinigen Tisch* restaurant!" tried another
one.

Daddy drove on without another word. He was
smiling just a tad. Everybody could see it, too.

"Now I know!" burst out another child. "We're going
to the Old Rhine for a walk!"

Well, at least, he had the right direction.

"That's right, but we'll stop here for a minute first,"
Ernie finally answered.

He stopped the car in the parking lot of the Old Rhine
Airfield. The weather was particularly nice that Sunday,
so things were quite busy. Soon, all six of them were

standing by the fence, admiring the small airplanes. The kids read the names printed on them. Ernie explained the different aircraft models to Hedi: Piper, Cessna and Bravo.

A gorgeous machine rolled out of the hangar. The door opened, and two people got out. For Ernie, it was interesting to watch the face of the pilot. He was carrying out his task with an easy confidence, almost smugly. He was master of the situation. The plane rolled out onto the runway, and off it went. All were turning to watch the shiny bird disappear over Lake Constance. In some faces Ernie could read amazement or admiration. Others showed a bit of envy. Still other faces reflected feigned indifference. Takeoff and touchdown, hello and good-bye – it was always the same.

The Tanner family just stood there fascinated. The only thing Ernie could think about was, "Will this be part of my calling one day? Will I be able to reach all those tribes this way? Where is the path leading now?"

This was not to be the last Sunday he would spend at the airfield. Sometimes, he would drive to Sitterdorf where there was a wonderful playground for the kids. The boys and girls had their fun, and Ernie could follow the events on the runway undisturbed.

Through an acquaintance, Ernie heard about a female helicopter pilot nearby. With great anticipation, he and Hedi drove to an airport restaurant to meet with her. He inundated the woman with questions. She could barely answer the half! While his meal got cold, it got warm in his heart as he heard about all that the chopper could do. As soon as he heard how much a pilot's license would cost–not to mention the maintenance fees for a machine– he had to "think again." It had been a noteworthy day but hadn't brought him much closer to his goal.

Ernie did not let himself be deterred. His heart's desire was to pave the way for the Gospel in Africa. He learned about a mission society in England which used aircrafts. Ernie contacted the director. He put him in touch with its founder, Steve Stevens. That same fall, he and Hedi set off again. It was very important to him that she be there. How else could she fully stand behind him? How else could she get the whole picture of all the steps yet before them?

They got a cheap charter flight, leaving for London early on September 18, 1970. The plane was jam-packed, uncomfortable and behind schedule. Nevertheless, they were full of expectancy. Would today seal their future? Was Steve the man with the solutions? Would the Missionary Aviation Fellowship (MAF) help them further on their way? Hedi was somewhat unsure as she looked around the plane. Everything was new and unfamiliar. The questions she posed to Ernie didn't have that much to do with Africa. It was enough for her to deal with the weather, the delay, the passengers and the British breakfast. Plus, she didn't know any English at all.

They met Mr. Stevens at the airport and took a double-decker bus through London together. It was a beautiful autumn day. They sat down on a bench at Piccadilly Circus, watching the pigeons and the traffic. Ernie presented his matter to the politely attentive Briton. MAF was using a lot of small aircrafts to make life easier for missionaries all over the world. For a long time, then, they talked about how their work was organized, about flying and about future options. They also discussed possible dangers, such as accidents occurring.

"Why not use helicopters?" The question had been on the tip of Ernie's tongue. "They are much more versatile."

Steve's answer was short and sweet.

"Helicopters are fantastic, without question. Nothing can hold a torch to them. Unfortunately, they are also absolutely unaffordable."

That was the end result of their London visit. Somewhat wiser, thanks to this disappointment, they returned to Trogen, Switzerland, the same day.

"Do you still believe you'll take up flying, Ernie?" asked Hedi.

"I do believe it, but I won't push it. If God wants me to do it, then I do, too. Otherwise, no way."

They had to return to their daily lives. There was no such thing as "boring routine" with the Tanner family. Every day brought something new. They were still building things. The old office had become too small. It was moved to a spacious room in an adjacent building. The two large windows there displayed a marvelous view.

Every morning, a family of deer would come up from the forest. There, they grazed peacefully, not a hundred feet away from them. From the edge of the woods, you could hear the rushing waters of the Goldach River down in the valley. A pair of gray herons had built their nest near there. Marcel always kept his binoculars close at hand. Every once in a while he would look up from his calculations to watch these seemingly proud birds.

Ernie made sure that he had a little podium in front of every window. Here, he could study and make plans. Here, ideas were birthed—and sometimes laid to rest again. Here, he prayed, sighed, groaned and rejoiced. On the big wall behind them was a map of Africa. Ernie and Marcel literally felt Africa breathing down their necks, continually coaxing, "Come back to help us!" This room was quiet, shielded from the busyness in the main house where people came and went. From here they kept in touch with many friends and acquaintances made on their trips. Some contacts were made through speaking engagements. Slowly, it became impossible to write each and every one individually. The idea came to create a newsletter for those wanting to support Helimission. Right from the beginning, it had a very personal touch. It also served as a means of keeping the large Tanner family financially above water.

In addition to the four children, Maria and Carmen lived with them in the house. Maria, who had come from the Black Forest, was the boss in the kitchen. Carmen wrote letters, and with her songs, added a joyful touch to the place. Wherever Ernie went, he invited people to come and visit them in Trogen. This place surrounded by nature seemed to be the perfect place to come to rest for many, especially the sad and troubled carrying great burdens.

Ernie called his house "Salem" because it was intended to bestow peace upon each visitor. Some would come and stay for a few hours. Others stayed for six months or even a whole year. During the summer holidays, it became hard to recognize the house in the open countryside. Thirty to forty kids would join the four Tanner children out front! Evenings at supper, there would be much laughter and singing, screaming and yelling, fighting and pushing at the table. Finally, each person would find a seat. "Uncle Ernie" then would shush everyone so he could say "grace." While everyone was busy eating soup, "Aunt Hedi" noticed little Urs sitting quietly, not touching his meal. She watched him for a moment. Suddenly, a big tear drop splashed onto the rim of the soup bowl. That was another thing which they had learned to deal with—comforting children missing home.

At night, Hedi was called to the bedside of little Gabi.

"I have forgotten what my Mommy looks like," she confided.

The following night, she said, "Mommy always tells me a story." In the end, "Mommy" had to come pick up her little homesick child. For the others, time flew by like the twinkling of an eye. The two weeks of camp were filled with singing and telling Bible stories, working and playing, making crafts and taking day trips. Many of the kids came year after year. They enjoyed being together for these retreats and were greatly blessed.

One day, Hedi was sitting in the living room, knitting and waiting. "Knitting and waiting" had become synonymous to her. Finally, the person she was missing so much entered the door. With great commotion, he was welcomed home. His eyes were glowing.

"Come into the living room," he beckoned his family. "I have something to tell you."

"Did you go to the Bear Caves of Bern?" The questions started again.

"Did you have an accident?"

"How long was the ride?"

"Simon wants to go, too!"

All of the children were shoving and talking at the same time.

"Well, let me start at the beginning."

Daddy was keeping them in suspense.

"When the meeting in Bern was finished, I drove up to Belp. There is a helicopter company located there. I could see their machines from far off. Kids, you know what?! It gave me goose bumps just to see them from a distance! But I really wanted to get up close to see the interior, at least once. So, I made my way over and found a mechanic happy to show me a small machine, a BELL G3. I stared at the seats, the stick, the instruments. After a while, I asked how much a short sightseeing trip would cost. Kids, I got to fly! For ten whole minutes I got to hover above the treetops and potato fields along the Aare River. Then, we remained in the air for a while. The motor was quiet as a mouse. The pilot began tilting the machine to the side, ever so slowly. Finally, he started a steep climb and then launched us forward again. It was fantastic!" Ernie was excited.

"It's exactly what we need in Africa! Exactly!"

In his mind's eye, he had already seen himself flying across the jungle, landing in the bush villages. Taking off. Landing.

"Let's pray, okay?" All of them bowed their heads, and their father asked his Heavenly Father for a helicopter. What a day it had been! But Ernie would still have to be patient. The year passed. Nothing seemed to indicate that God would open a door in this direction.

Meanwhile, the Tanner children did receive a big surprise! On December 30, their youngest brother Lukas was born. The two girls had wanted a sister; the two boys, a brother. The mother and father's only concern was that it be a healthy baby. Early in the morning, they had sneaked out of the house to go to the hospital. When Aunt Nelly woke up the kids, they all knew what was going on.

"Did Mommy go to the hospital?"

"Is it a boy or a girl?"

In the afternoon, all of them went to the hospital and marveled at the "tiny boy." The midwife laughed and told them he was really a big baby! Hedi and the new family member returned home six days later.

The atmosphere was a bit strained when she returned home. The time was approaching for another trip to Africa. Saying farewell had never been easy, but this one was doubly hard. It weighed heavily upon them. Ernie did not say a lot. He prayed for his family, commending them into God's hands. Then, he hugged each one of them, pulling them tightly to his chest. He kissed sleeping Lukas on the eyelids. Then, he got into the car, which was packed to the uttermost limit. Immanuel, as the oldest, was allowed to go to the airport with him.

Chapter 10
Auntie Nelly

Hedi had grown up in a little village of one hundred souls. For as long as she could remember, she had lived in the school building where all the village kids were taught. At night, she could hear the comforting rush of the Rhine Falls nearby. Hedi had always felt safe there, even when heavy thunderstorms were passing over.

Aunt Nelly had been a school teacher there for forty years and also lived in the building. Hedi's mother had been divorced and tended to her sister Nelly's household needs. Hedi would pitch in. Whenever she would appear in the village store with her shopping basket and list, old Mrs. Fischer would always say, "Well, well...here comes our little Hedi!" She loved and appreciated Aunt Nelly more than anyone else. She was there to comfort her when her doll's dress had gotten torn. When the neighbor kids laughed at her, she was there to wipe tears away. Sometimes, Hedi was even allowed to sit in Aunt Nelly's classroom although she was only five years old. Aunt Nelly was very smart and knew a lot about a lot of things. In difficult situations, she would always make the right decision. At the time, Hedi didn't know about the tears Aunt Nelly would cry in secret. After five years in Zurich, Hedi returned to the Rhine area. Only then, "wiser with age," did she begin to see into her aunt's heart.

Hedi went on to attend the high school in Schaffhausen. There, she faced many negative situations. She could, however, always count on Auntie to help turn things around. In her living room in that school, Nelly always had an open ear for her niece. It was no wonder, then, that Hedi felt drawn to children and, eventually, the teaching profession. During her training in Zurich, her aunt was the one who stood by her side. The first letter she wrote after final exams was, of course, to Aunt Nelly.

Hedi knew that no one could understand her as well as she could.

It was simply natural then that once Aunt Nelly had stopped teaching, she would move in with her loved ones in Trogen. There, she shared the joys and sorrows of the young family. It was also Aunt Nelly who, for many years, was a financial blessing to the missions-minded Tanners. Advanced in years, she often reverted back to her old "schoolmarm ways," much to the "joy" of the Tanner children. Still, she was very loved and admired in Salem.

Chapter 11

"Hotel Bravo X-ray Delta Kilo, Come in, Please."

Springtime brought Ernie and Marcel back to Switzerland in one piece. They also brought a great piece of news back with them. During their difficult mission in Cameroon, Ernie had shared his concept of using helicopters several times in public. Björn Bue, a Norwegian, was one of the ones who listened most intently. He was the director of a national project sponsored by the Alliance brethren, entitled "New Life for Everyone." He had given enthusiastic vocal support to Ernie, assuring him that his idea could be the fulfillment of a dream. The more Ernie thought about it...the more he asked God for confirmation...the more convinced he became: it was time to take action. He wrote about it in his next newsletter, urging friends, acquaintances and even distant on-lookers to support them financially in this venture. He closed with a strong word, challenging people to step out on the water:

> Why should we be toiling like Livingstone and Stanley when the best technical capabilities are at our disposal? The time has come to make use of this modern tool on the mission field. People may criticize me all they want. "I am prepared to go on foot, but I am also prepared to take the higher route. Have you ever walked through the hot jungle with blisters on your feet? Have you ever shared your bread with mice? Ever been eaten up by scores of mosquitoes? If not, please reconsider your judgment of me...."
>
> If everyone would give one-tenth of his savings toward this, we could fulfill the dreams of many missionaries by putting a helicopter to use. Should we really allow finances to hold us up in this

endeavor? Never! If everyone would just give his five loaves and two fishes, we'd surely have twelve baskets left over. It is well-known that God does not build His kingdom where there is abundance; rather, He takes what little we have and works with it.

In 1971, the signs of spring took their time in coming. Thick fog lingered over the hills of the Appenzellerland. If you looked hard, you could still make out Ernie Tanner driving his Peugeot regularly from Trogen toward Altenrhein. At the airport, he got out of his car, and, taking a deep breath, stretched a bit. Then he would march over to the airport control tower building. Every flying lesson would cost him, not just a great deal of concentration, but also absolute self-control. When he would come home three hours later, Hedi would study his posture. Usually, she could tell if the lesson had been a success or not.

"How did it go today?"

If no reply came, she would try again, "Was your instructor happy with you?"

Ernie would sit down at the table in the living room, tired. He would look outside where the air was still frosty and sigh.

"I feel much safer on the ground than up there!" he admitted. "Landing is just terrible. The guy's always criticizing me and making fun of me. If I didn't know my reason for doing this, I'd give up for sure. Every time I attempt my final descent, he screams at me, 'Mr. Tanner, don't just sit there all bent over the stick! You are much too stiff. Mind the angle of approach! You haven't got it, yet.' After that, *of course*, I flew much too close to the rooftops! And I didn't turn where he wanted me to."

Hedi hardly knew how to comfort her husband, usually so strong and determined. Every flying lesson on that plane was a nightmare for him. The little red Piper didn't even let him rest at night. One time he woke up bathed in sweat and groaning. He had just crashed the machine in his sleep.

One morning, Ernie made a surprise announcement. "If the weather is clear enough today, Hedi, I promise you'll get an eyeful for a change! I'll fly over our house and circle 'round."

This was a promising development. Ernie left, summoning up new courage. Not half-an-hour later, Hedi heard a familiar humming sound up in the sky. She stood in the middle of the playground, heart thumping, and waved at him with her red headscarf. Slowly, the small Piper came closer. To think, her Ernie was up there, flying that airplane! She was fascinated. Now, he turned the aircraft around at an angle. He was actually looking at her. Then, he tilted the machine to the right and then to the left several times in a row as if waving with the wings.

"Hey, that's a pilot's greeting. I remember him telling me. Ernie is a pilot! I can hardly believe it!"

For a long time, Hedi remained there, trying to grasp what effect this would have on her life. It was not the first surprise in thirteen years of marriage. For now, she would just have to put the thought out of her mind without understanding the ramifications of it.

Ernie had dared to take the first step. Now, nothing would stand in the way of him realizing his goal. Before the children's summer retreats, he would have to travel to America.

"Daddy is going to bring home a real helicopter!" one of the kids yelled at his departure.

He laughed as he said good-bye. *How* he wanted to accomplish that would remain his secret for a while. It took several weeks, but then Ernie called with triumphant news.

"Hello, Hedi, my sweetheart!"

He sounded out of breath with excitement.

"I've found a helicopter, a BELL 47J, a red and white four-seater. It's a wonderful bargain. We'll only have to put twenty-five percent down by July 31. We'll get that together, I'm sure. God will help us with it, and so will our friends in Switzerland. Hedi...are you still there? What do you say? Fantastic, isn't it? I'll organize everything for the transport and come home. Everything's going to be all right, my dear! Don't worry!"

Hedi's enthusiasm was lagging behind Ernie's. Time and time again, he had had to encourage her in her faith. If he had just been riding some wave of enthusiasm, Ernie Tanner would surely, at some point, have succumbed to all of the adversity gathering on the horizon. But his child-like trust in God was unshakable. It helped him overcome one hurdle after another.

Upon his return to Switzerland, the first line of business was passing his fixed-wing flying test. Time to grit his teeth once more. Ernie arrived at the Altenrhein Airfield on July 22 with butterflies in his stomach. Deep down, he also felt hopefully curious. How was God going to help him get through this day? He boarded the aircraft with the examiner. He determined to leave the flight instructor–and his cutting remarks–way behind him on the ground.

"Well, Mr. Tanner," the man with the clipboard began, "we are going to have a wonderful flight together. The weather is all for you."

They did, and it was. For the very first time, Ernie felt pleased and confident during the whole flight. He was not disoriented at all. The examiner chatted with him in a friendly, casual manner, as if they were driving down the highway. Ernie had expected things to go well. Still, when he passed the exam with flying colors, he felt like he had been given a huge gift.

Another highlight followed. The down payment for the helicopter came together on time! God was the one who'd initiated this plan; now, step by step, things were falling in place. As soon as summer camp was over, Ernie traveled to Bern to be retrained for flying helicopters. He found a competent coach in Mr. Demuth, who worked for the helicopter company. Ernie took an hour lesson in the morning and another one in the afternoon. He simply couldn't get enough. He finally sensed he was getting closer to his goal and to his calling. Soon he knew every hill and valley, every village and stream, every road and every bridge surrounding Belp Airfield. He got to study them from a bird's eye view every day. It didn't take even three weeks until he had the helicopter license in his pocket.

A course in radiotelephony followed. In order to fly, you must be able to communicate with air traffic controllers. You must know pilot language, especially the "alphabet." As soon as he'd gotten started, Ernie would practice whenever the Tanner family would take a drive. The license plates of cars coming out of Zurich, that is, from the opposite direction, were now called "Z-H, Zulu Hotel."

Even the kids joined in. "There is a car coming from Thurgau!"

"Tango Golf!" Immanuel shouted.

"Excellent!" his daddy would praise him. "You'll be flying soon, too!"

"Yeah, flat on his face," was the answer from one of his siblings.

In the meantime, the helicopter was on its way across the ocean. Getting it through customs was a bureaucratic nightmare. It took hours on the phone and miles on the road, not to mention mounds of paper to get everything settled. Ernie crossed each bridge as he came to it, signing papers in his usually friendly and patient manner. When it all got to be too much, the grumpy side of Ernie would show its face. The officials in Bern could not understand how someone could buy a helicopter without having the slightest clue about terms like "A-check," "external landing permit," "TO," "ROD," "FPM," and "DH," to name a few.

Finally, the machine was in the country. It was being assembled at the helicopter company in Belp. Now all it was missing was a name. The Swiss aviation department had to make that decision. Then the letters could be painted on its side. The chopper received the registration, "HB-XDK" or "Hotel Bravo X-ray Delta Kilo."

Chapter 12
The First Flight

"The news that our chopper had arrived in Kloten triggered jubilation in all of us," was how Ernie described his emotions at the arrival of his long-awaited, prized possession.

He could hardly get to Zurich fast enough to admire the parts still wrapped in plastic. They all would have loved to have taken it home right away. First, it had to go to Heliswiss in Bern for assembly.

Soon, it was finished–a glorious bird to fly. It just so happened that, with this model, the pilot sits in front by himself. All three passengers sit in back. Initially, Ernie did not give it any thought. When the time came to "spread the wings of this pretty bird," it dawned on him that he would be flying without an instructor at his side. He describes his first flight attempt like this:

I wasn't familiar with this model at all. Plus, I had only had thirty lessons before taking my exam. Now I, a rank beginner, was supposed to take to the skies?! My heart was beating like crazy. The steering was, in principle, similar to the machine I'd learned on. The instruments on the dashboard were arranged differently, however. Under the critical eye of my instructor and the Heliswiss staff, I fastened my seatbelt. I tried my best to look calm but was trembling inside. My heart beat even more loudly until I could feel it in my ears. The engine came alive, making a crackling noise. Then, the rotor blade began to turn. I was facing a great test of courage.

I had barely left the ground when the machine swept me upward at an amazing speed. A deep layer of clouds hung over the airfield. I wasn't prepared for the significantly higher velocity of this machine. It was quite a shock. Everything was going by so very fast. Suddenly, the clouds under us were racing toward me, and I disappeared into the white fog. Panic-stricken, I pushed the stick forward. Immediately, the machine responded, taking a nose dive. Promptly, I saw land below me again. I was approaching the farms down there at the same speed. So, I hoisted the machine back into the fog right away. It went on like that for a couple of times. Finally, I got that crazy thing under some kind of control. I shuddered at the thought of flying that unruly machine to Africa. I couldn't get back to Heliswiss fast enough, hoping there would be no surprises during my landing. It went well. When I got out, the earth seemed to tremble beneath my feet.

A few days later, it was time to fly our HB-XDK back to Trogen. Marcel Gasser and I went to Belp by train. He was very calm, which was a great comfort to me. I was so glad I didn't have to take this on all by myself.

Spotlessly clean and all tanked up, there she stood in the hangar. Beautiful...that's what our machine was. Only the pilot was missing. Nervously, I checked the machine and said good-bye to my instructor, Mr. Demuth, as though I were about to take off for a routine flying lesson. In truth, my stomach was churning. The tower gave clearance for takeoff. This time around, I held the "reins" tightly right from the start, not allowing my two hundred and forty "horses" to dash off like that again.

It had snowed since my last flight. Everything was covered in white. The world looked altogether different. It was a cold day, too. We had barely left Belp for Trogen when I noticed a warning light had come on. Gently, I made an adjustment, moving a lever down. If the preheating were done too suddenly, little ice particles could come loose, blocking the fuel's passage to the carburetor. I still remembered that from flying airplanes. My eyes were glued to the warning light; it simply didn't want to go off. I pushed the level down further. Mercilessly, the light stayed on. A feeling of panic wanted to grab hold of me. I kept circling around, in order to fly to Belp, if necessary. Where were we, anyway? We had paid so much attention to the heater that we had lost our orientation. Why did everything have to be covered with snow at this time, anyway? Even the roads were barely visible.

I pushed the heater lever down even further, but the light still did not go off. It stared at me defiantly, as if wanting to say, "Enjoy your final moments of life. The engine will kick off by itself!" Fear paralyzed my thoughts and movements. Back to the airfield—as fast as possible! But where was it? Behind us? In front of us? To the right or left? While I radioed the airfield, we tried to figure out in which direction we would have to fly to locate Belp. My tone of voice probably sounded as if we were practically dead already to the air-traffic controllers. We got immediate clearance for landing. But *where* were we supposed to land? It seemed as though the lamp were shining all the brighter.

Finally, we could see the villages, the Belpberg mountain and the sorely needed airfield. Would we make it? Yes, we would. Mr. Demuth was there, waiting with some mechanics.

"What's up?" he voiced with concern. I told him.

"Well, why didn't you push the lever all the way down?" he asked reproachfully. "That's no reason to lose your nerves!"

With these words, he yanked the heating lever down and sent me back up into the air. The horrifying light had disappeared almost immediately. Of course, this went against all the regulations I had learned flying fixed-winged machines. But this was a *helicopter*, and I still had to get to know it much better–with much fear and trembling.

Trogen was easy to find. First, Ernie flew a circle around Salem. Then he prepared for landing, his first historic landing, behind their modest house. There they were, all of them–Hedi and the children–to welcome Ernie and his venerable bird home. Soon, Helimission would be writing history.

Chapter 13
Donations for Aviation Fuel

For the Tanner family, things would never be the same. It seemed as though the previous forty years had only been "batting practice" for Ernie. Now he was stepping up to the plate. It was a God-given assignment. God did not call specialists for certain tasks, Ernie would say, since specialists are usually confident in their own abilities. He was sure of one thing, "God couldn't find a simpler person, so He decided to take me."

For six weeks, the helicopter stood parked behind the family's house. Occasionally Ernie had to return to Belp to iron out one glitch or another. Some neighbors were quite shocked about having a helicopter in the neighborhood. Others were rather pleased. It just depended on who was being allowed to fly along or not.

Christmas time had come. Instead of preparing for the holiday season, Ernie was studying maps. He brooded over the Mediterranean Sea and North Africa, determining distances, calculating flight times and comparing route options. He did not consult any professionals; he consulted God. He needed permits for flying over land as well as for landing, data about airfields, and, of course, fueling stations for aviation fuel. At all times, Marcel was his constant and willing helper, adviser, and sometimes correspondent. He typed away on his typewriter for hours, producing one letter after the other. Some were informative. Others were thank-you letters. Others may have had a justifying or even begging tone to them!

Preparations were being made not only in Trogen. Different missions in Cameroon were also getting organized. The Norwegian Lutheran Church, the Apostolic Church, the Basle Mission and the Presbyterians—all were expecting the helicopter in February or March. Together with indigenous evangelists, these missions wanted to take advantage of the dry season to buzz into faraway bush and mountain villages. They wanted to minister to the people there–many waiting with anticipation–before being picked up by the helicopter again. The African believers received special training for just this purpose. Trogen and Cameroon sensed a special connection: excitement and expectation ran high on both sides. It was a risky venture–a venture of faith.

Ernie began the new year with his same kind of inquisitive, expectant attitude. What would it bring? He had sent a letter about the upcoming mission to all of his friends. He had enclosed an aviation fuel booklet consisting of bank transfer slips. Those who received his letter were to use them to make donations for aviation fuel. He had also kindly asked the recipients to remember his family during his absence. He had no time to worry about finances. He simply cast this care upon his heavenly Father.

On the morning of January 17, the entire Tanner family and all their fellow-laborers met together in the living room.

"Today, our little helicopter will embark on a great journey," Ernie said. "Whenever possible, we will call at night. Later on, we'll send telegrams since there won't be many possibilities to make calls. We think we'll get to Cameroon through the desert. We'll see then and there how that's going to go. Now, let's pray together. We'll be meeting every morning at God's throne, as in the past. Is that a deal?" Then he prayed.

The chopper stood ready for takeoff in the snow behind the house. Prior to departure, Ernie had gone through the regulation checkup step by step. Then he and Marcel boarded the machine. The turbine engine came to life. The rotor blades began to move, spinning ever faster. Gently, the helicopter lifted off, hovering above the ground for a moment and whirling up a lot of snow. Then it gained speed, flew in a circle to say farewell to those it was leaving behind, and disappeared on the western horizon.

On February 10, Hedi wrote to the friends who supported them:

> Dear Friends,
> As much as I would like to write each one of you personally, I simply cannot. However, please receive my gratitude as if I were with you because it comes directly from my heart.
> At 12 p.m. on February 2, our two pioneer missionaries finally landed in Cameroon. They had been flying through spacious, rocky regions and desert-like areas for over two weeks. At this point, I have not yet received word as to which mission they will fly first. Rest assured that it'll be just like at home: they'll have no time to write.
> In closing, let me say thank you once again for your aviation fuel offerings as well as for your donations for those of us staying behind. We are interceding for you without ceasing.
>
> With loving greetings,
>
> Hedi Tanner

A little later she wrote again:

> Dear Friends,
> I've received joyous reports concerning the various bush missions. My husband has written in every single letter how full his heart is of praise and thanksgiving for all he is experiencing. He has emphasized how much he is striving for total dependence on God in everything. He covets your prayer support. He's also been making lots of progress as far as flying is concerned, he has

written. Thanks to his compass, he has been getting to his destinations very quickly. Things have been working out well with the refueling, too.

Up until this point in time, they have set up bases in four regions of eastern Cameroon. From these, they then fly out to the remote villages. He has received all kinds of offerings so far: a cross made of flowers, fruit, chickens, goats and even two live crocodiles. Starting March 6, they'll be visiting more unreached villages in the remotest areas of western Cameroon. Accompanying them will be Otto Tanner. March 20 is the date set for their return flight. I would like to earnestly solicit your prayers for that time.

I thank you for all your love gifts from the bottom of my heart. My very best wishes to you.

Yours faithfully,

Hedi Tanner

Chapter 24
I Get to Know Fear

It didn't take long for difficulties to arise. At the outset of the trip, low-hanging clouds right outside Belp blocked the view, making navigation a challenge. Ernie followed the railroad tracks down in the Black Mountain Valley, that is, until they disappeared into the mountain. He made a turn and tried to leave the valley through a hole in the clouds. All of the valleys and villages looked alike! It was very disorienting. Finally, he landed on a field and asked the surprised farmers where he was. Still in Switzerland! And already lost! What was it going to be like in the desert then? For now, Ernie and Marcel did not worry about that part. The immediate question was how to get to Geneva. From there, they would follow the Rhone Valley all the way to the Mediterranean Sea.

As a precautionary measure, they flew down into the valley and followed the highway. They were flying very low to be able to read signs. Suddenly, Marcel let out a yell. Ernie had already pulled up the machine. An electric cable had suddenly appeared before them out of the fog. The men had gotten the shock of a lifetime. It had been a close one. Marcel quickly glanced around, making sure the landing gear would not get caught up in the wire. The excitement was only beginning.

At Cointrin Airport they refueled, called home and took off again. The closer they got to the Mediterranean Sea, the stronger the wind would blow. They got to know the mistral, a cold northerly wind whistling down the Rhone Valley. The plan was to refuel the machine in Perpignan.

Ernie's face had a look of determination as he maneuvered the stick. He was busy with both his hands and feet, trying to keep hold of the reins of this whirlybird. It felt like it was doing a wild dance in the air. The force of the gusty wind often buoyed them up to dizzying heights before dropping them into an air pocket again. The rotor blades rattled so loudly that Marcel was afraid they would not be able to withstand the enormous pressure. Neither he nor Ernie spoke a word. The two were focused one-hundred percent on their flight path. Ernie followed the coastline, hoping to meet calmer conditions. He was wrong! Things got even worse. He tried to fly at a lower altitude. Even then, the helicopter was being tossed to and fro. He had no other choice but to land carefully on a field partly covered with snow. From there, he radioed the nearest control tower and waited for better weather.

The flight along the Spanish coastline turned out to be very impressive. On their right, they could look far into the country. On the left, they could see the horizon, where the sea and the sky touched. This view from behind the spherical Plexiglas was breathtaking to the inexperienced pilot and his assistant. They calmed down, refreshed by the beauty, and gathered courage again. They flew over one bay after the other. Marcel identified the villages and towns using the map spread out in front of him. He also fed the pilot in front of him dried fruit.

"Ladies and gentlemen, we are arriving in Malaga," Marcel announced cheerfully.

"All right," Ernie answered, not as thrilled. "I can't wait to get to Gibraltar so we can cross over into Africa. Slowly but surely, I'm getting tired of looking at all this water."

They reported to the tower of Malaga Airport. The controller welcomed the Swiss helicopter. He reminded the pilot that, from now on, he would have to keep a seven-mile distance from the coast since this was a prohibited military zone.

"Just what we needed!" Marcel heard his friend sigh into the headphones.

Another critical phase was beginning. Ernie pointed the chopper toward open sea. Those seven miles were quite a distance from the mainland. Only by flying at a very high altitude could they still see the coastline.

"We are flying at 190 degrees, Marcel. Please check quickly whether we can reach Morocco this way. It's directly opposite Gibraltar!"

"It's 98 miles as the crow flies. Do you see the ship down there? Wouldn't it be better to fly in an arch, parallel to the coastline? We'll see the Rock of Gibraltar from far off. We could use it as a landmark."

"Good idea. Keep your eyes open and pray that we don't fly past the Atlantic."

After that, the only thing they could hear was the deafening sound of the rotor blades. It made them tired after a while. The visibility was getting worse by the minute. The clouds were getting lower, too. The small helicopter seemed to be seeking comfort from the white waves below them.

At the coastline of Africa, another horrible surprise was waiting for the two men. In Tetouan, the first airfield on African soil, they received disappointing news. The mechanic told them the aviation fuel had already run out for the day. He suggested they go to Al Hoceima, "only" an hour away. Ernie and Marcel looked at each other and then at the fuel gauge.

"Do we have enough?"

"It's going to be tight."

"Well, we'll just have to get there. No one's gonna bring us any fuel to this forsaken place."

They checked out all other possibilities. They put their heads together with the few people working there. They bought something to drink before returning to the chopper. All was silent for a moment after they had gotten on board.

"Should I go ahead, Lord?" Ernie buckled up and put on his headphones. "Ready for takeoff," Marcel heard him say.

The engine started and the striped bird shot up simultaneously. Soon, they had reached the coastline. The blue water appeared friendly and calm. Foamy waves came crashing down on the shore. Ernie thought about home. He'd been gone for a week already. Had Hedi received his last telegram? She wouldn't be worrying now, would she?!

"I'm glad she doesn't know all the details," he moaned to himself. Then he snapped out of it. He had to concentrate on the task at hand. "How far is it to Al Hoceima?"

"We've made it halfway."

"What a desolate place this is! No roads, no houses, no life!"

"Oh, but there is something. Look down there!"

What was it? Something was moving in the water. Ernie dropped the bird down a bit to see more clearly. Two huge fish were actually swimming in front of them. They were literally racing through the water. Ernie checked the fuel gauge instinctively. No emergency landing now, please, with rocks to the right and sharks to the left, he thought. He accelerated.

"We ought to see the town pretty soon. Or else we'll be out of gas."

Both of them scanned the horizon in desperation, seeing nothing but mountains, rocks and water.

"My dear Heli," Ernie spoke out loud one of his nicknames for the chopper, "show me what you are made of. You can do it. Get us there, baby!"

The engine droned on. Eventually, the coastline disappeared below them. Their eyes burned from looking so hard. Ernie began perspiring.

"Don't lose hope," he told himself. "Keep your head together. Those sharks can go look for dinner somewhere else!"

With only four gallons left, they landed at 11:06 a.m. at the small airfield of Al Hoceima.

The beautiful flight along the Algerian coastline was followed by a cold and snowy one across the Atlas mountain range. The two pioneers would not let the stressful conditions deter them from their destination. Three days later, they had reached the heart of the Sahara: Tamanrasset. Under their Plexiglas dome, the heat was scorching. Now, they had to battle to keep their concentration. Finally, Ernie was able to land his faithful whirlybird on the desert airstrip. Both men got out of the helicopter with "relief" written all over their faces. They stretched their stiff legs and arms a bit and started looking around. Another airplane had just landed. A small group of passengers had gotten off and disappeared through a gate. Now, what?

Ernie gathered his thoughts, looking at the helicopter.

"A checkup is due after one hundred hours. Do I still remember how to do that?" He bent down slightly and looked at the belly of the bird. "That's right. I've got to loosen this big bolt right here. I need a wrench for that and a bucket...."

He looked around. Not a soul to be seen. What should he do? Pondering a moment, he walked up and down.

"Lord Jesus, I am in the middle of the desert. Please help me."

Then he looked up. A man was sitting on a fence some distance away in the direction he was looking. Ernie walked up to him, saying hello in English, and asked if he knew where to get a bucket and a wrench around here. The man stretched his legs and got up from his seat.

"Well," he said in English as well, "what do you need a bucket for?"

"I'm flying that helicopter over there. I need to do a twenty-five-hour check."

The stranger came to life.

"What kind of an engine is it?" he asked, very interested.

"A Lycoming."

"Wow, that's great. I'm a Lycoming mechanic. I'm working for an oil company over here."

Off he went to get the needed tools.

"You say you come from Switzerland? I am an American. Here's what you asked for. Do you want any help?"

Ernie's heart leapt. For a moment, he stood there watching the man from the side as he got to work. Was he truly a mechanic—or was he an angel? Why had he been sitting there on that fence? Had God placed him there just for this dilemma? Marcel and he paid attention as the man carried on as if everything were second nature to him. Ernie could even recall every single point to check off that he had learned at the helicopter company in Belp. This had to be the best experience in the desert thus far.

Now, they had to get things organized for their upcoming flight. Ernie went into town to look for a vehicle to transport the aviation fuel barrels. He finally located a Land Rover and a driver. The next task was to find some barrels. That took two days. At night, the driver would bring the vehicle to a meeting place. There, he would wait for the helicopter, all tanked up, to show up the following day. They had enough fuel to fill up the chopper a second time after about 217 miles. That would be enough to take them to the Agadez Airfield 601 miles away. This procedure repeated itself many times. The challenge was always whether or not they would find the Land Rover again. Not only did they find the vehicle, but they also managed to make their way through the unending Sahara, picking out the right route from many in the sand.

Ernie decided not to send a telegram home from Agadez. He would probably be back home before it arrived. He continued his journey and that same day reached Zinder, a city in the south of Niger. In years to come, he would have some very unpleasant experiences there. Ernie and Marcel spent the night in a simple hotel.

They woke up early and left without breakfast while it was still dark.

They looked forward to Nigeria and other inhabited areas. There they would have rivers, roads, villages and railroad tracks to help with their orientation. The tension finally eased off a little. On February 1, they reached the Atlantic Ocean in Calabar. Flying around Mt. Cameroon, a mountain with an elevation of 13,123 feet, they landed at Douala International Airport at 3:38 p.m. The next day, they flew on to Yaounde, their final destination. They had spent a total of sixteen days—or sixty-two hours and forty-one minutes—in the air.

Chapter 15
It Was All Worth It

It was time to send a victory telegram home. Ernie had made it. At times, the goal had looked so far out of reach, even in his eyes. He had always approached things from a practical angle, though, leaving the theory to others. This attribute had helped him overcome seemingly insurmountable obstacles. Now it remained to be seen just how much good their new missions tool could bring.

Ernie's friend, the Norwegian missionary Björn Bue, had gotten him a flight permit. He had been dreaming about a possibility like this for a long, long time. Together, they wanted to put their ideas into practice. They flew across the impenetrable wilderness called the jungle. At times it looked like a thick green carpet below them. They discovered small villages at the Gabon border, where they preached and proclaimed the Good News. The helicopter was, at the very least, a good tool for drumming people up wherever they landed! Avid listeners were to be found in many places. In addition to sharing the Word, the missionaries dressed wounds. They gave advice for planting crops. They helped in matters of hygiene. They were up from morning 'til night. In the first six weeks of his helicopter mission, Ernie learned more about Cameroon than ever before.

His cousin Otto Tanner, the head of the Kumban mission, had looked forward to hosting Ernie for the second half of the stay. One of the places they visited together was Ngwandi, a village located high up in the mountains. Back in 1969, they had hiked there on foot. On their short flight, they crossed familiar valleys and looked down over those steep mountain slopes. The jungle paths did not lead up the mountain in a leisurely serpentine path, like in the Alps. Instead, they went straight up to the peak or the ridge. The weather had been so hot and humid. They remembered groaning under their heavy loads—and being very thirsty! What a difference between the short flight and that six-hour march! This time, they arrived strong in body and joyful in heart. They talked with the villagers, learning more about their problems, and helped them as best they could in all areas. They preached a Gospel message and returned to the mission's headquarters in Kumba the same day.

Marcel, Ernie's faithful companion, was busy with his medical supply chest. He would bravely wash out and dress extremely putrefying wounds. His other duty was to have the video camera ready. They wanted to show their friends back in Switzerland the highlights. He quickly picked up what the indigenous people were saying. This meant he could also understand Otto when he spoke to them. For example, Marcel wanted to videotape the black cook at his house.

"You be tie your face proper so," Otto reprimanded the cook. "As you tie face proper so, I sabi say you be no saved man at all." That meant as much as, "Don't make such a long face. If you do, I am sure no one will think you are saved."

You see, to the Africans, being taped was serious business. When the camera was pointed at them, they wanted to look solemn and sober!

Ernie and Marcel also heard other expressions several times a day. For example, "Today it be hot plenty pass number," which amounted to, "Today, it is hot beyond measure." Another phrase was, "Me, I get longer throat pass you all," which meant, "I am thirstier than all of you put together."

Those phrases may sound funny in the ears of foreigners, but there is not much room for gaiety or laughter in the life of Africans. Fighting for survival is too hard, and the future, too unsure. Therefore, the tremendous change which takes place when they accept Christ is very apparent. They clap their hands and dance. Their faces shine as they sing songs out of the depth of hearts which have been set free. The external change even carries over into their environment; that is, their clothes are cleaner; their homes more orderly. Their immediate surroundings simply become more attractive.

March finally arrived and the rainy season was close at hand. Ernie made preparations for his return flight. He carried out a thorough checkup on the machine. Then he said farewell to Cameroon.

On March 20, Ernie and Marcel left for Douala and returned through the desert again. Instead of flying past Gibraltar, however, they chose the route via Tunis, Sicily, Rome, Genoa and Locarno. At the Swiss embassy in Tunis, they picked up the inflatable rescue boat which had been sent there for them. It was quite a moment as the small helicopter with two Swiss men in life jackets left the North African coast behind them. For one very long hour in the air, they saw only sky and water. At such times, the temptation is great to get lost in your own thoughts. The key, however, is not losing sight of your destination. With a focused quietness about him, Ernie remained on course. He watched his compass closely and listened to the sound of his engine. He fixed his gaze on the horizon, keeping an eye on the wind and waves. Oh, how they looked forward to seeing land behind all this fog! What a great relief it would be! And so it was. They finally had something to talk about again. Four hours and twenty minutes later, they reached Palermo. The following day they made it to Rome without difficulty.

On March 31, they crossed the Mediterranean Sea once again on the way to Genoa. Then, the engine began to make a knocking noise. Soon, it seemed to be coughing and gasping. The mysterious sound really jarred Ernie. He looked at the gauge; they still had plenty of fuel. What could be causing it? Ernie radioed the tower in Genoa and described his problem.

"You are not far from us. We have you on our radar already," came a reassuring reply. "Stay on course and begin your descent. And stay in touch."

"Thank you. I can see the coastline already," Ernie answered. Then he and Marcel began calling on God for help. The engine's sputtering became even more irregular. It sounded as if it could die any moment now.

"Hotel Bravo X-ray Delta Kilo, continue giving us your coordinates! Stay on course for a direct approach. We are keeping the control room free for your landing."

The man in the tower kept speaking encouragingly to them. Ernie was, by now, bathed in sweat. His hands were dripping, and he felt like his heart was in his throat. The soothing voice helped him put the machine securely on the ground.

"Marcel, we're safe!" he whooped. He got out of the bird, thankful to be back on solid ground!

They discovered that the engine had overheated. The contacts of two spark plugs had melted. Two of the six pistons were not working any more, which caused the engine's sputtering sound.

At 10 o'clock on the morning of April 1, the telephone rang in Trogen.

"Hello, Hedi! Hotel Bravo X-ray Delta Kilo and its crew have landed on Swiss soil again. By the grace of Almighty God, Marcel and I have arrived in one piece in Locarno. How are you and the children?"

"How wonderful to hear your voice! We are very well. You know, I received a telegram yesterday, dated January 24, from Oran, Algeria, saying you were okay. That was a real April fool's gag! The next one will probably arrive in summer."

Hedi laughed, very happy.

"And how are you two desert foxes doing?"

"Oh, you'll see as soon as we have crossed Mt. Gotthard. The weather is not cooperating too well on this side. We'll try it anyhow. Give the children my love. I can't wait to hug you–tonight."

At 1 p.m., a second call came in.

"Since Mt. Gotthard was too foggy, I tried another route but had to give up after an hour. It was impossible to get through. We had to turn back. What a shame! So close and yet so far!"

Hedi had to sleep by herself for another couple of nights. On April 3, they finally celebrated their reunion. Four days later the helicopter had to be flown to Belp where it would be chartered for the summer months.

Three months had passed since the chopper had left Trogen. Twice, it had taken sixty hours to cross the Sahara. In Africa, fifty hours had been spent flying to deliver help to various places. Was it all worth it? After this first "heli-mission," there was no way to measure the results with pen and paper. What it did mean was that a new era in missions history had begun. Taking on a new frontier meant making investments. Investments in time...money...energy....

Chapter 16
Wolf

"Never again will I fly the XDK to Africa!"
Ernie was spouting, releasing the pressure that had built up during the past weeks.

"It's just not good enough. The trip was one big experiment–much too dangerous! Only God Himself kept us safe and brought us back home unharmed. Since He was the one who put this dream into my head and brought it to pass, I'm sure I'm on the right track. Now, don't get worried, Hedi, but we're going to buy a Jet Ranger. And don't ask me how or with what because I don't know yet. But you'll see!"

Hedi was totally speechless. A Jet Ranger! She knew enough to know that that modern, orange helicopter was one powerful machine. In her eyes, it had one major disadvantage: too expensive! Even now, people were envious of Ernie. Some were openly critical; others criticized his plans in secret. Some even warned him "kindly," patting him on the shoulder. They said being adventurous was fine and good, but all of that money could be put to better use elsewhere. He'd better think of his own family. He himself had plenty to do in Europe. Was it all actually worth it?

"Who is that sharp-looking pilot taking off in that orange machine over there?" Ernie asked a mechanic close by, fully intrigued.

"He lives in Samaden but was born in Austria. If you ask me, he's the best helicopter pilot I've ever seen. He flies for some stinking rich Greek man."

"Yeah, you can see it in his step. Man, he lifted that wild whirlybird off the ground as if it were light as a feather! He just hovered for a second, and off he went!"

Ernie was dreaming out loud.

"A Jet Ranger...that's something else! What a difference from our puny one! I'd love to have one like that."

"Mr. Tanner, if I am not mistaken, it's up for sale."

"Really? Do you have the address of that man?"

Ernie drove home. The piece of paper with the address of Wolf Weinlechner in Samaden was burning a hole in his pocket. It was almost as hot as the note that had led him to the French-speaking part of Switzerland way back when. Ernie could hardly wait to tell his wife about it. Did this fellow really want to sell his machine? Was it in good shape? Most certainly. He had seen that baby take off–live and up close!

Ernie came home and told Hedi the story. He made the call immediately.

"Well, what did he say?" Hedi was curious right away.

"He wanted to know some things about us, who we were and what we are doing. He wanted to talk to his boss since he can't make the decision himself. His boss is not around at the moment but will be coming back from Greece sometime soon. He'll contact us once he has spoken to him."

It did not sound very promising, but at least it gave them time to take the whole thing before God in prayer. It also gave them time to save their bills. The money was not enough for a Jet Ranger yet, but maybe the rich man could wait a little.

The Tanners took heart. It did not take long until they heard from Mr. Weinlechner: the machine was really up for sale. Someone else was also interested, but his boss wanted to meet with Ernie. Would he come to St. Moritz?

The smell of fall was in the air. The good old XDK, called Delta Kilo, had spent the summer in Greenland. Now it was coming home. It had served many hours, earning its owner good money. Happily, Ernie counted it out. It looked like enough for a good down payment. He,

with Immanuel as company, drove to St. Moritz with a
bank statement tucked inside his breast pocket. He had
also taken a videotape about his work in Africa with him.
Both of them were full of excitement at meeting this rich
and important man.

First, they met with Mr. Weinlechner whom they knew
from the phone calls. Immanuel was especially thrilled
at meeting this famous pilot. Then, with expectations
soaring, they drove over to his boss. The meeting went
positively, and the parties reached a decision quickly.
The gentleman agreed to take the down payment and
wait until next fall for the rest. Ernie and Immanuel
returned home ecstatic. In September, Ernie would
return to Samaden for three weeks. Mr. Weinlechner
had offered him lessons on the new machine as well as
special training for high mountain altitudes. All of that
for free! It was hard to believe, but true....

Meanwhile, there was no lack of visitors at the house
in Trogen. Summer camps and weekend retreats—a
constant coming and going of people from near and far. Life
was never boring for the Tanner children. Hedi, however,
could hardly cope with the stream of visitors. How often
was she tempted to let out a sigh of exasperation! Yet
she vented those "sighs" by keeping a journal. Soon it
was time, once again, to say farewell to her husband. She
sensed a bit of fear trying to nag at her. She watched as
he waved good-bye, full of high hopes and maybe even a
hint of well-deserved pride. Then his car disappeared,
heading for Samaden. She went back into the house and
looked out the window to check on the children. As she
turned around, her eye caught sight of a Bible verse she
had once written down ages ago: "I will both lay me down
in peace, and sleep: for thou, Lord, only makest me dwell
in safety—even when I am alone." Today, it brought her
comfort again.

In Samaden, a new adventure in the flying arena
began for Ernie. His 240 flying hours on his good old
"J," another nickname for the first chopper, did not really

help a lot in his test flight. The Jet Ranger was a wild whirlwind which, at first, seemed to have a mind all its own. Usually the instructor was patient, explaining its various functions in detail. At other times, however, he would suddenly lose his cool and start cursing. Shocked, Ernie would then really mess up! For hours, the helicopter would make its practice rounds in the beautiful Engadine region. Ernie learned to maneuver more confidently every day, taking on ever higher ridges. In the end, he even dared to venture up as high as the Bernina peaks.

"It's hard for me to keep flying with you, Wolf," Ernie said one day to his astonished instructor.

"How come?"

"It hurts me too much when you use the name of God in vain, you know?"

"Okay, I'll try to work on that."

At night, the pilots would get together to sit around with friends. As is the custom, they would swap "war stories," sharing about accidents and near-accidents they had had. The language was quite dour. Suddenly, Wolf slammed his fist on the table.

"We have a pastor in our midst. He can't stand all this cursing, so cut it out, all right?!"

Turning to Ernie, he whispered, "I've done much better today, haven't I?"

When the orange XCX chopper, "Charlie," had landed in Trogen after thirty-five practice hours, it was time to celebrate. To say thank-you for the many lessons, the Tanners invited Wolf and his wife Mariann out to dinner. Here, they were no longer instructor and student. It was the beginning of a real friendship which would stand the test of time. Wolf was never more than a phone call away. His advice would get Ernie out of a jam more than once. Even a million dollars could not cover what Wolf's support would be worth in the following years.

Part Three

Chapter 17
Stuck in Constantine

"Practice makes perfect," the old saying goes.

It is certainly true, particularly when applied to flying. Ernie took those words to heart. Despite his Africa journey, he still had only 275 hours on record. To stay on top of things, he used to take every possible opportunity to get that orange bird up in the air. Of course, it would have been a "sin" to fly alone! Many of his friends, relatives, acquaintances and neighbors had the pleasure of joining him on his training flights–not to mention the children, who loved flying the most!

The helicopter carried them all over Switzerland. Ernie had gotten used to flying there quickly. The world certainly looked different from a bird's eye view, especially when covered with a white blanket of snow. Yet finding his way was definitely easier than flying, as such. Even so, every takeoff seemed like "stepping out on water" to him. Later, looking back in hindsight over all the difficulties, he deduced, "Faith without risk is no faith at all!"

One of his favorite passengers was his brother Jacob. Many years had gone by since their childhood days. Since then, "Jack" had become a company photographer for a big enterprise. Ernie and he rarely saw each other. When they did, they would start reliving sibling scenarios the second they got together.

"Remember how we gave it to those 'city slickers'?" one would start.

And so it went. Both would remember different aspects; for example, the look of surprise on the boys' faces...untying the little kids...running for their lives... claiming victory with a shout!

"You were pretty nervous, weren't you?"

"Me? No way. You nearly wet your pants!"

They were very graphic in recalling the details. It was clear the brothers thoroughly enjoyed "the trip down Memory Lane."

It was no stretch, then, when someone suggested they do something together again. Why didn't Jack grab his camera, for example, and join Ernie on a trip? The two debated all the pros and cons. In addition to snapping photos, Jack could videotape events and help however else needed. It didn't take long for them to agree on making the voyage of the Jet Ranger to Africa together. Everything was meticulously prepared; the dates were set. Both of the Tanner families in Trogen and Uzwil were busily getting ready. Marcel, Ernie's right-hand man, was to take a Swissair flight this time. For the return flight, Jack and Marcel would trade places.

The first day of the new year had come. It was time to take leave of their families. The XCX was in top form. An additional fuel tank would relieve them of having to work with spare cans. This way they could fly from one airfield to another in the desert. They had their flight maps, flight permits, passports, vaccination cards, logbook and camera all ready. In prayer, Ernie committed themselves and this flight into God's hands once again. Then both brothers kissed their wives and children good-bye. Off to Samaden! The weather left something to be desired, but they made it to the Engadine region safely. They were glad to spend one more night on Swiss soil.

Jack recounts the unforgettable impressions of this flight himself:

It was 1972. I took a once-in-a-lifetime chance to join Ernie on this flight onboard his Jet Ranger. Preparations began the summer before our journey. We got our vaccination shots for cholera and typhoid fever. We purchased a new camera. Everyday matters, such as food, clothing and accommodations, were not of much concern. We researched two possible routes, one via Italy and another via Gibraltar. Ernie decided the shorter one from Palermo to Sicily and across the Mediterranean Sea would be better. Heavy thunderstorms in Spain and a low-pressure system over Corsica caused us to make a detour around the entire zone. We saw the Alps to the left of us.

The two attempts to reach Genoa, Italy, from a low altitude were really dangerous. Power cables would often pop up out of the fog when we were only thirty feet or less away. It took all of my brother's flying expertise to avoid them without an accident. In fact, at the time, I didn't know how really dangerous it was. However, I still let out a sigh of relief when we reached the Adriatic coastline. We could even identify fishermen and shell collectors below us. They put their fishing poles down to wave at us!

Our target destination for the day was Bari. There we wanted to fill up the tank and spend the night. Twilight made things difficult, though, not to mention the fuel gauge, which was slowly approaching empty. We were forced to fly to Foggia Airport which, unfortunately, was a prohibited military zone. The only visible landmark to help us were the lights of the city of Foggia. We thought about how nice it would have been to have a hot meal and cold drink in one of the nice restaurants below!

Ernie tried to contact someone at the tower of the military base. There was no reply. Who would be concerned about some low-flying object suddenly appearing in the evening sky, anyway? When Ernie finally yelled, "We don't have any more fuel. We have to make an emergency landing!", someone finally answered softly in Italian, "Where are you?" We had just enough juice left to find an open spot before the helicopter touched down on soft soil.

Thirty minutes later, headlights appeared on the adjacent road. Police officers, holding flashlights toward the right and left of our bird, were yelling, "Helicottero, Helicottero, Helicottero!" The first couple of policemen were not the last ones to question us either. One insisted upon knowing our grandmothers' first names.

Ernie was taken to the city in a military jeep to get something to eat and find somewhere to sleep. To be on the safe side, I stayed and took a nap in the cockpit. However, I was not going to be allowed to stay by myself for very long. Around 1 a.m., I heard a soft knock on my window. When I opened my heavy eyelids, I found a thermos can being offered to me right outside the window. A very short man was holding it up. He was barely tall enough for his hat to reach the bottom of the window. In his other hand, he was holding some sandwiches. My sparse knowledge of the Italian language was not enough to describe my feelings of gratitude. The look in my eye was unmistakable; in fact, it didn't take long for us to understand each other. It was a delightful experience for both of us. I loved the warm, sweet coffee with milk and delicious big French bread. He loved talking to the "major captain" of the helicopter. He asked me to send his children a postcard from Africa. He scribbled their address on a piece of toilet tissue, content to take his leave.

After a short, uncomfortable night's "sleep," I was awakened by several policemen at early dawn. All of the men on duty through the night wanted to be there for takeoff. Therefore, twelve officers were standing in a line on the field–up to their ankles in mucky mire. It was only with maximum turbine velocity that Ernie could lift the chopper out of the sticky mud. Overnight both skids had sunk deeply into the soil due to the heavy weight of the machine. It was 6 o'clock on the dot when our helicopter bid farewell to the policemen animatedly waving at us. A good flight and a wonderful night's rest in a warm hotel bed in Palermo made up for the night in the cockpit.

Thereafter, we found ourselves very close to the shore of the Mediterranean Sea. We landed there briefly to see to the final preparations for our flight to Algeria. My brain will, for the rest of my life, probably never experience such overload as it did in those few minutes. Weeks before the trip, Ernie had explained the procedure for an emergency landing on water. Now we had to recall the steps as we watched the sky wrap itself in a cloak of pitch-black clouds. Nothing, however, could stop us from finishing what we had started one week earlier.

We put on our life jackets. Then, Ernie bowed his head and said his usual prayer. As copilot and not as strong of a believer, I doubted whether the Man Upstairs really was concerned about our flying project. Only a short time into the flight, the storm broke loose. The sky was dark as night. The wind produced waves twenty meters high, which seemed to be touching the bottom of our chopper. Desperately, Ernie kept trying to correct our course. I, in the meantime, used tissue to stop cracks in the window caulking. The storm was doing its best to force the heavy rain through every cranny. To be on the safe side, Ernie tuned in the emergency frequency on our headsets.

We were in the middle of the Mediterranean when our conversation was suddenly interrupted by a loud voice. We could hear the voice of another man in our headsets loud and clear. He was curious to know more about us.

"Hey, who are you down there?" the voice boomed. "With whom do I have the pleasure of speaking in this remote place?"

At first, I thought Ernie was talking. I looked at him, but his lips weren't moving. It had to be the pilot of another machine flying above us. He introduced himself as "Tango" and said two other words. He was flying at 36,000 feet above sea level directly above us on his flight from Zurich to Tunis. Ernie told him briefly that we were on our way to Constantine in Algeria and, as a result of the weather, were about three hours late. Then, he asked this friendly comrade if he would use his much more powerful radio to contact Constantine Airport about our delay.

The kind voice wished us all the best for our further journey. In this deserted place, hearing the comforting voice of this pilot–talking in a Swiss-German dialect from home–seemed like being in a fairytale. It also helped to know we were on the right track. It didn't take much longer for the thick, black curtain to open up above us. There it was... a clear, blue sky. The sun was even shining on us. The long-awaited view of the bay with its prominent mountain welcomed us. Ernie laughed. He said he knew we would be all right. After all, a bunch of people had been backing us up in prayer.

So, by some miracle, we were now flying over the coastline of Africa. I had been eager to set foot on the Black Continent, even though much of what I had heard was not so uplifting. Africa was the place where a child died of hunger or sickness every other second. It was the scene of many religious wars with innocent victims. It was the final stop for many courageous missionaries.

Then, there were villages filled with strange people, peculiar traditions and unusual religions. Strange, to us. Yet it was also a continent of diversity with unique rainforests, lush jungles, beautiful mountain ranges and indescribable deserts.

I had so been looking forward to seeing those black faces with their glowing eyes. Before I would have the pleasure, though, we would get to know Algeria better than we would liked to have. At first, we were relieved and glad as we began our descent. After all, it was an important stage on our flight to Cameroon. After we had taken the final mountain ridge, the city of Constantine unfolded before us in the evening sun. A city of contrasts, it featured state-of-the-art skyscrapers, interesting mosques and an awful slum area. There was also an impressive river flowing through a deep canyon which, for millions of years in time, had been making a serpentine path through the rocks. For both of us, it was breathtaking. We were speechless. After all of the difficulties and bad visibility while crossing the sea, I, too, was more than happy to have made it here safe and sound. What remained ahead for me, though, was the fear of crossing the great Sahara.

It was nighttime. After a brief customs check, we were taken in for interrogation by the police. We had to fill out many forms, the last one being pink. It was a permit which allowed me, a tourist, to take pictures. It was a good idea in principle; practically, though, a policeman in the city wouldn't accept its validity unless he had put his John Hancock on it personally! Go figure?!

A short while later, we returned to the airfield to check out what kind of shape our Charlie was in before making the long flight across the desert. Ernie was as smooth as a professional. Even I took a hard look at our whirlybird, and something caught my attention, a small hole. I asked Ernie about it. Could it be dangerous since the casing was already dented as a result of the enormous pressure conditions? Ernie was shaken to the core. Horrified, he said that we could by no means continue. The rotor would have to be replaced. But how? We could only find another one in Switzerland.

If the tail rotor, moving at great speed, had broken off on one side, the chopper would have been thrown out of kilter. It would have kept turning on its axis, going faster and faster. We would have been forced to land on water quickly. That would have been the worst-case scenario. The pilot would have been forced to eject both doors and, simultaneously while tilted, let the main rotor destroy itself on the surface of the water. This is to avoid passengers being hit by the turning rotor blades after jumping into the water. The copter would only stay above water for a few seconds. The passengers would have to exit fast as lightning to avoid being drowned with it. With waves several feet high, it would almost be impossible to be rescued alive. The freezing cold water temperatures would have made survival tough, too. No one would have seen us, and there probably wouldn't have been enough time to radio SOS.

What followed had become fairly routine to Ernie: return to the hotel and try to reach someone at Heliswiss on the phone. Ernie also tried to contact them by fax. It was a Saturday, so usually no one would be working. A mechanic answered.

"You mustn't fly under any condition," he warned. "The rear rotor has to be replaced. We'll send you an entire set since you won't be able to balance the rear rotor down there."

Ernie was astounded. That bad? It was only a small dent. You could hardly see it!

"Go ahead and send a mechanic as well," he replied, disappointed.

"Okay, we'll call you as soon as we get a flight out to Constantine."

"Please let my wife know that we are stuck out here."

The first thing Hedi wanted to know was whether anyone had been hurt. Then, she asked how much the repairs were going to cost.

"Well, the damage won't be more than 10,000 Swiss-Francs," the caller comforted her. For Hedi this was devastating news. The helicopter hadn't even been paid off yet!

There was heavy snowfall on Monday morning at 6 o'clock as we stood waiting at the airport for the mechanic to bring the rear rotor. The Air Algier twin-engine propeller machine landed on time. A young man jumped out and hurried over to meet us. He held a mysteriously wrapped package in his hands. In freezing temperatures and in the dark, he set to work on our beloved Charlie with no gloves on. Not an hour later, he was finished. We gave him a hug, got into the helicopter and flew out of Algeria as fast as we could.

On the fifteenth day of their journey, Ernie and Jack arrived in one piece in Kumba. Cousin Otto was waiting for them. Everyone was elated, feeling a great weight lifted off of them. They thanked God for bringing them there. They were grateful for being granted another opportunity to share the Gospel. Marcel, who had flown commercial, was also there. He was a great help to Ernie in overcoming bureaucratic hurdles. The key word: wait.

"Come back in the afternoon."

"The boss is in a meeting."

"There are new forms to fill out now."

"Wait for the signature of the top man."

In the meantime, Jack used the time to pursue a hobby. He captured the shiniest bug he had ever seen for his collection. Then he caught the most colorful butterfly of his life while "waiting" in Otto's garden.

Chapter 18

Bamenda

Otto had done excellent work in preparing everything in advance. The helicopter was on the go for two weeks straight. Every day Charlie flew to three or four villages, carrying indigenous evangelists and nurses as passengers. In one or two weeks' time, they would be picked up again. The names of the villages sounded rather funny to Ernie's ears: Banga, Kumba, Noian, Manjemen, New Difenda, Ifanga, Small Buto, Mbu, Lipenja, Ekondo Titi, Ndian, Obanekan, Nguti, Mosongi, Oban, Bamenda. It was nearly a miracle that he would get the right people to the right place at the right time and then pick them up at the right place, too!

Bamenda, located in the northwestern part of Cameroon, was the starting point for the missions that followed. The town had an African hospital, a bank, a post office, stores and many governmental office buildings. It also had a huge market place which would fill up with people. The crowds could only be compared to the size of those in a soccer stadium at home.

Bamenda was also home to several different missions stations. Who would have thought back then that Helimission would set up its base there as well within a couple of years? Situated at about 4,200 feet above sea level, the climate there was much more pleasant in comparison to hot and humid Douala. Many missionaries would come here for a vacation. Therefore, Ernie, Jack, Otto and Marcel were able to stay at a guesthouse for missionaries. It turned out to be a suitable starting-off point for their flights. Their itinerary was brutal, if you could call it an itinerary. Often their passengers were not at the meeting point. Sometimes sand clouds would prevent them from seeing anything. At other times, they had to respond to an urgent emergency call.

A special task was waiting for Ernie in Balin: a bush hospital was to be built. Balin, a very small village, could be reached from Benakuma; it took three days through the jungle. The path led through the territory of the Essimbi tribe. Other native African tribes were afraid of them. This made it very hard to find people to carry construction material and hospital beds there. Ernie decided to attach the loads to the copter and fly them over in several half-hour flights.

He knew a very brave woman there who had marched into Balin years ago, taking only the bare necessities. Since then, she had been living and working with the Essimbi. Her name was Marga; she was a German nurse. It was a special pleasure for Ernie to help her. Part of the building material was already waiting in Benakuma. It took six flights to carry the boards, nails, tools, iron-cast bed frames, windows and doors into the wilderness to Balin. Marga was overjoyed at their arrival. In her mind's eye, she could already see the bush hospital finished. She was the only nurse within a fifty-mile radius. During her walks through the area, she had made a map and drawn all the paths, huts, and villages of this area. Using her sketch, she explained to Ernie the best route to take.

Marga didn't talk much and laughed even less. Her facial expression was very strict. Living alone and seeing such need had left their mark on her. At some point, Marga had taken in six orphaned girls to care for.

Every year thereafter, Ernie would visit Cameroon. He would make a point of flying to Balin. He was delighted to help support the bush hospital. Ernie would bring Marga everything she had ordered the year before. Nowadays Helimission pilots fly to Balin every month. Although Marga is no longer there, two of her adopted "daughters" care for the sick at the bush hospital. Once in a while, a doctor is flown in to help as well.

Chapter 19

Marcel's Statistics

While Ernie was flying here and there, Marcel also stayed very busy. He would fill up notebooks with facts and figures, just like at home. On location, he would add names, dates, flight times and miles flown to his long list of statistics. He would also ask the Africans before a flight how long it would usually take to go by foot to their destination. The natives were pretty good at estimating. The days and hours they quoted were backed up by grueling marches under the tropical sun. Ernie and Marcel had experienced firsthand what it was like to keep up with an indigenous guide over mountains and through valleys.

The results Marcel came up with were mind-baffling. In forty-seven flight hours, they had flown to fifty-seven places. The estimated distance they had flown was about 5,300 miles. At a speed of 1.8 mph, that would make 2,825 hours. Had they walked for five hours a day, it would have taken 565 days...more than one-and-a-half years! The helicopter, on the other hand, only needed nine days under the same conditions—it was sixty times faster. More importantly, the missionaries could save their energy and protect their health. The data gave Ernie a boost. They warmed his heart more than words could have expressed. His aim was not just to aid the poor in preaching the Gospel by word and deed, but also to help other missionaries. He wanted to make things easier for them, thus multiplying their ministry. He had written these goals down in the statutes of Helimission.

Statutes, however, are just paperwork. Marcel's statistics were cold and lifeless. Standing behind Helimission were many people with warm, generous hearts of flesh and blood. The results produced through their show of love could not be evaluated by tables, facts and figures. Who can measure the worth of one single person coming to Christ? Just as a person who has been rescued from a life-threatening cliff-hanger never forgets his rescuer, a human being who has been saved for eternity never forgets the one who showed him God's love. This is true success.

Chapter 20
Charlie Won't Fly

Every time Ernie would fly supplies to Marga, he would cross an area where the Essimbi were living; at least the natives told him so. With every flight, Ernie felt more strongly drawn to these people. He would keep an eye out for their huts or villages. He often checked to see if there were a place to land. On his last flight, he decided to give it a try. He hovered over a grassy knoll. Marcel jumped out to flatten the high grass a little for the chopper. Then Ernie landed, switching off the engine. Total silence. Time to wait. After a while, they heard voices coming from the bush. Soon enough, the first natives appeared. Ernie climbed out of the helicopter. He walked toward them, stretching out a hand to the first man.

"Hi," he said loudly, "How are you?"

"Welcome," the man replied.

The second person also greeted him, "Welcome."

One after the other they came out of the bush. After all of them had gathered around the copter, Ernie tried to explain to them both in English and with much signing why they had come. They promised to return with a doctor for the sick among them. The Essimbi listened and nodded. Ernie and Marcel got back into the bird, waving at them and telling them to step back. He tried the ignition, but the helicopter wouldn't start! Everything they tried was a waste of time. Charlie wouldn't budge.

So they got out of the machine again. They had no other choice but to stay in the jungle—no matter how tough it seemed. The bush people quickly understood their situation. They easily comprehend situations before a word has been said. They can read facial expressions and sense whether a person has good intentions or not.

The Essimbi returned by the path they had come, allowing Ernie and Marcel to join them. After climbing up and down hills for half an hour, they finally reached the village. Everyone sat in front of their huts until nightfall. Then some women prepared a meal of rice and fish. They all sat there for a long time. The pilot and copilot were far from any city and far from any road. They were in the middle of a village; the inhabitants had chosen a very limited area to live in. It was as narrow as the valley spread out in front of them.

Finally, the chief arose, fetching a lantern. He beckoned Ernie and Marcel to follow him. He led them to a hut and pointed toward a wooden frame with a simple, "Sleep here." They lay down on the boards used for a bed. It was still very hot, so sleeping was hardly an option. Later on, some men climbed up a type of ladder to the "second floor" of the hut. It didn't take long for the missionaries to hear snoring. It got on Ernie's nerves, so he tried to sleep outside. There, he was victimized by flies and pigs.

At daybreak, he returned to the helicopter. Maybe Charlie had changed his mind. All efforts were in vain. In his opinion, the problem was the starter-generator. That meant heading back to those huts. Ernie and Marcel shared a bit of breakfast, the last cup of malted milk and a banana. Three men were sent to Balin. They were to take a letter to Marga and bring back a few important things, such as water filters, tools and food. Ernie took the starter-generator with him. He headed out for Benakuma to telephone from there.

The chief offered Ernie his own small son as a guide there. The boy took a step toward him, observing him with keen, solemn eyes. The path led from one Essimbi village to another. Sometimes, they would receive a warm welcome; other times, hostile eyes would follow their every move. Ernie was very glad to have his small black friend with him. At every stream, the boy would jump into the water to refresh himself. He eagerly drank of the refreshing water while Ernie took only a sip of water he had brought in a Coca-Cola bottle. He simply knew too well how dangerous it would have been for him, as an European, to drink from those African waters. The heat really got to him. He was sweating and wheezing. With every hill, his pace became slower, and he stopped at every stream for a few moments. In one village, he bought an unripe pineapple to quench his incredible thirst. Hours and hours later—he no longer cared to keep track—they reached Benakuma. In a small restaurant, he drank almost half-a-gallon of mineral water but did not eat anything. He said good-bye to his companion, giving him a nice reward for his help.

Then Ernie inquired of one of the locals if he could rent any means of transport—car or bus or bush taxi? They did not have those here.

"That means walking again," he sighed.

"No," said the man, "I've got a bike."

They made a deal, and Ernie borrowed the old, trustworthy bicycle. After riding for about an hour, he saw a white man sitting outside a hut.

"Hey, what a surprise!" he cried.

"The pleasure is all mine!" the man replied in French.

Upon hearing Ernie's plight, he offered to give him a lift to the main road on his motorbike. It was getting dark by the time they reached a building next to that lonely stretch of road. Cars were nowhere to be seen. The owner of the small bar told him a bush cab would be going to Bamenda at six o'clock the next morning. Then, he was given a place to sleep. Ernie barely had enough strength to thank God for all the help. His thoughts returned to Marcel who was still with the Essimbi tribe. He also thought of his family back home.

"Keep them safe, faithful Lord, because I sure can't!"

The next day Ernie finally found a telephone. He called Hedi, and, once again, it was wonderful to see how well they could work together. Everything came together like clockwork. Heliswiss had the right starter-generator in stock. One of the mechanics knew "by coincidence" that one of Ernie's good friends would be flying out to Cameroon that very week. That meant Ernie would receive the much-needed part in four days' time. The helicopter remained stuck for exactly a week in Benabingo, an Essimbi village. During that week, Marcel lived with the bush people and went hunting and fishing with them. Ernie found both Marcel and the chopper in good shape upon his return.

When departure time finally came, Ernie had flown over that mountain range again and again. He had had to cross over it on foot two times. He had been dripping wet with sweat! He gratefully and respectfully patted Charlie, his "faithful horse," on the instrument panel. From then on, he was sure to keep him "fed" with the best kerosene fuel possible. Never had he appreciated his good friend as much as now!

On March 30, Ernie finished his second helicopter mission. In those 155 flight hours, he had taken indigenous and foreign preachers, medical personnel and government officials to the remotest of places. In addition to transporting food and medicine, he had also brought supplies to the bush hospital. Ernie had already gotten used to extremely strenuous missions. Now he was getting a good grip on flying. With a sense of satisfaction, he and Marcel got ready to fly home. Seven days later, they reached Switzerland without any problems.

Ernie had taken the XCX back home, intending to make it available for charter flights during the summer months. He had hoped to be able to pay it off through the revenue. That did not work out. No one seemed to need a helicopter. Thus, Charlie waited patiently in a temporary hangar in Trogen.

During that time of financial uncertainty, Ernie received a letter from Cameroon. The news didn't just bring joy to his heart, it also confirmed the path he had chosen. An American doctor was working at the Donekeng Hospital in Bafia, Cameroon. His wife had written Ernie:

> My husband is a surgeon, and I assist him as a nurse. We are the only Caucasians in a hospital with one hundred and forty beds. We had already visited many villages but were limited by transportation. We could only go where our Land Rover would take us on these awful roads. This year, as one of five teams in our district, we were asked to participate in the helicopter mission. We were skeptical as to the efficiency of this method, but we agreed to go along.
>
> We heard of one man who ran through the jungle for days to inform the respective villages of our coming. Then, while putting a cast on someone's broken leg, we suddenly heard a helicopter above us. We grabbed our supplies and ran to the machine. All of our stuff made it on board: medication, instruments and even a pulpit for our services. Just a few minutes later, we headed off to the mission's headquarters. With our Land Rover, the ride would have taken nine hours, wearing us out. Now, we made it in only fifty-five minutes. Quite refreshed, we landed in Yoko.
>
> From there, the helicopter flew us to the first of three villages in the deepest part of the jungle. At first, we only circled above the huts. All of their inhabitants hid from us. Then the pilot found a spot to land. Soon, the natives came out to welcome us. For two days, we worked there, examining and treating all the villagers. We also were able to hold services before the chopper picked us up

for the next village. Today, we are persuaded that the helicopter is an enormous tool in bringing help to those in need. Some wouldn't receive help any other way. We are already looking forward to the next mission.

Dr. and Mrs. Sandilands

Chapter 21
A New Door Opens Up

This year, the day of departure was scheduled for the fourth of January. A DC-6 from Balair stood ready at the Basle-Muehlhausen Airport. The Tanner children watched spellbound as an orange helicopter disappeared into its big belly. Although their noses and feet were freezing, they would by no means miss watching the supplies being loaded. They also stared at the television crew videotaping this event. Daddy was not just leaving home: he was boarding a large machine this time. It seemed it would swallow him up out of their sight, just as it did the chopper. They stayed back by themselves in the cold. Finally, the hustle and bustle came to an end. They stood looking at each other, a sinking feeling in their stomachs. However Mommy was still there. She took Simon and Damaris by the hand.

"Come on," she smiled. "Let's go home to Lucky. Daddy will be back soon."

They turned around to leave. Immanuel and Miriam followed more reluctantly. That month, Hedi wrote a letter to their friends and mission partners. She described the running around and sleepless nights prior to Ernie's departure:

When God wants to do something wonderful, He usually allows some difficulty to get in our way at the beginning. If He wants to so something "especially wonderful," He'll allow us to have to tackle an impossibility. In our last newsletter, we mentioned only briefly that a new door to Ethiopia had been opened. We did not know what we would find behind that door, but God had already gone ahead, preparing everything perfectly.

On December 22, Ernie Tanner was sitting in his office, writing down the schedule for his helicopter flight to Ethiopia via Greece and Egypt. Then he received a message that really took the cake. The Sudan Inland Mission (SIM) wanted to pay for the flight of a DC-6 from Basle to Addis Ababa. In return, we were to load our helicopter into this DC-6 and load it up with desperately needed relief supplies for this mission. My husband hung up the phone, and I heard him let out a holler, overjoyed at what God was doing! To our financial situation at the time, I can say it was difficult. We were having to stand in faith for more funds just to make the normal Helimission budget. Now we saw God making provision for us.

One phone call triggered another. Not every one of them was good news, but each one brought us closer to our goal. A few days later, we had experienced a small landslide. A German mission agency for the blind pledged 20,000 Swiss-Francs to help. An aid agency of the Evangelical Church of Switzerland (HEKS) had pledged the rest, which was about 13,000 Swiss-Francs. Between December 21 and January 4–and everybody knows how hard it is to get anything done then– we put this money to use in buying the following: two generators, one compressor with accessories, one welding apparatus, one underwater pump with hose, and one Theodolit, that is, a measuring device. We also obtained thirty manually-operated pumps from Vienna, thirty camping beds and sleeping bags, car tools and various other items.

The Red Cross donated woolen blankets, fifteen tents and three tons of powdered milk. At this opportunity, someone from that organization also thought up an invention: a drilling system for water wells. The idea was made reality through the selfless efforts of J. Wyssen of Reichenbach, Switzerland, and with advice from leading geologists. He and his two sons really put their shoulder to the wheel, building the drilling device over Christmas in their factory. Thank God, when they tried it out on New Year's Day, it worked! On January 4, the apparatus left for Addis Ababa onboard the DC-6.

Dear friends, everyone knows that all this would not have been possible without God's help. We want to give Him all the glory. To all of our missions friends, we would like to say thank you very much for your wonderful, generous and spontaneous support. Every franc is a great help in implementing the helicopter. Everything went well regarding the flight and assembly of the helicopter in Addis Ababa. To find out what happened thereafter, please read the report about Dessie, Ethiopia, which you will find below.

Dear Mrs. Tanner, dear friends of the Helimission,

In front of me is a geographical map of the Wollo Province. It looks like the mountain tops of the range on the western border of the East African Graben Valley are all covered with snow. They reach up to 14,055 feet, but this is an optical illusion. It is quite impossible to have snow at a latitude of eleven degrees north of the equator. If you fly to the east, it only takes about half-an-hour by helicopter to reach the desert. There, the Danakil Nomads live.

The Wollo Province is twice as big as Switzerland. In the past three years, we have worked with the government to send a health service team from the Sudan Inland Mission to the province. This area has barely been developed in Ethiopia. On account of our efforts, leprosy checks are now being carried out regularly at sixty-four farmers' markets. Eye medication is also being distributed. In addition, we've been providing clean water, especially for schools. Our hunger aid relief programs have been published in the media as well.

Dear Mrs. Tanner, we would like to thank you and your five children for doing without your husband three months in a row so that Mr. Tanner can assist us. Through his support, we can help relieve the needs of the bodies, souls, and spirits of about 3.5 million people in our province. The enormous extent of the work of your husband and his team with the Helimission Helicopter HB-XCX probably cannot be grasped in Europe. There, people can get into automobiles, onto trains or even board planes so readily.

Since the arrival of the Helimission team, we have been able to do more in one week than we would usually have done in two months. We visited various famine-stricken villages with four teams from the German Agro Action Group, part of a world hunger relief organization. We located sites for digging wells. We also found sites suitable for the construction of dams for irrigation purposes. We visited deserted villages and remote refugee camps. In addition, we were able to fly to farmers' markets which, prior to this, had been inaccessible. This was an encouragement to our Ethiopian staff members, whom we could also provide with supplies. We treated many people with eye disease. We were also able to preach the Good News of new life through Jesus Christ to the people.

What was it that suddenly made our work so much easier? Usually, it would have taken four hours to cross one of the deep valleys of the Ethiopian Plateau by mule. It only took five minutes by helicopter. We could reach a village with a marketplace in only seventeen minutes from our mission's headquarters. It would have taken a whole day by mule. What normally would have been a five-day journey–to reach a certain medic and his fellow-worker, an educator and evangelist–did not even take forty-five minutes. What a blessing to be able to do all this with much less fatigue and exposure to disease! So now you can see how we could accomplish more in one week than in two months! Utilizing the helicopter makes the hard work in this African Tibet almost feel like vacation. I was able to re-establish contact to our Ethiopian co-workers who, prior to this, had had to hold down their posts all alone in remote places. I feel as if a great burden has been lifted off of me. I shall never forget the joy I sensed watching hundreds of people, young and old, running up to the whirlybird. Many received help for their physical ailments. Many listened in concentrated silence to the Word being preached.

I must thank you again from the bottom of my heart for making this mission possible. Rest assured that our prayers are with you.

Best regards,

Dr. Dietrich Schmoll

Thanks to "Charlie," the XCX, twelve airstrips were either built or reconstructed so that the work with regular airplanes could be resumed. Wells were drilled in six strategic places with the newly invented drilling device Ernie had brought over. Three of these wells were found in refugee camps run by Germans. Beforehand, they had had to draw water from foul-smelling wells.

Our Swiss helicopter was not the only one running missions in Africa: four German, one French and two English choppers also did their part. Thanks to them and the support of many others from all over the world, much was done to relieve the great poverty of Ethiopia. What a joy to see fresh water springing out of the heart of the earth! Just as wonderful was providing heavenly water at the same time—the kind only available from the source of eternal life, Jesus Christ.

The mission into the Danakil Desert where the Nomads lived was a success. The helicopter transported food, medicine and seed for planting. It also took teams of doctors, researchers, missionaries and government officials to their destinations.

One missionary working in the southern part of the country shared his heart with Ernie. He knew of a minimum of ten tribes who had never heard about the love of God. He pleaded with him to bring his helicopter to help reach those people. This cry resounded strongly in Ernie. He took it home with him and never forgot it.

Chapter 22
The Swiss Ambassador

It was the beginning of March. After a tight, two-month schedule throughout needy areas, it was time for Charlie to make the flight across Africa to Cameroon. Many were waiting for him and his "master." The previous year, they had been able to utilize the helicopter to the maximum. From the beginning, it had been Ernie's desire to send it in where no other means of transport were possible. In Sangmelima, south of the capital Yaounde, for example, a number of teams from a Presbyterian mission were waiting to be flown into several bush villages. They preached about Jesus' love, nursed the sick and taught hygiene and horticulture. A few days later, most of the teams, consisting of natives, were headed for home again. Just like the year before, Bamenda was one starting point for their missions. Another one was Yoko; there, the Norwegian Lutheran Church was organizing trips.

After those three long months, Ernie was really missing home. His good old XCX couldn't fly fast enough for him, nor could they take bureaucratic hurdles quickly enough. In Tamanrasset, they had to wait two days for a permit to fly over land. While Ernie "gathered dust" in the waiting rooms of several offices, his copilot Paul wandered through the desert town. He wanted to take snapshots of interesting sights. One day, he seemed to find absolutely nothing to shoot during his walk.

Ernie had just returned to the hotel room, slightly disgruntled with all the waiting, when Paul appeared also, out of breath. He threw himself on the bed.

"We're finished!" he groaned. "They've got me!"

Gritting his teeth and frowning, he got up again. Then he looked around helplessly.

"Ah, it's nothing. They won't find me!"

He opened the camera, changed the films and put them under his pillow.

"Tell me what happened, will you, man?" Ernie was losing his patience.

They could hear men talking nervously in front of the building.

"Here it is. Here!" one of them yelled.

They stopped in front of the first hotel room and knocked. Silence. Ernie strained his ears. It was the police!

"Paul, are they looking for you? Where did you go?"

"Into town," Paul whispered. "I took a picture of a woman."

"Where?"

"In a yard. Very posh house. She screamed and then she disappeared. Then, these people came. What a drag!" Paul mumbled.

The voices in the corridor were coming closer. Now someone was banging on their door.

"Police. Open up!"

Ernie had no choice but to open it. He stood in the doorway.

"What's going on?" he asked in French.

"We are looking for a white man. He's got to be here!" the police said.

"Just a moment."

Calmly but firmly, Ernie did not allow anyone past him. First off, he wanted to know what had happened. He learned that Paul had stepped through the gate of a rich man's house, which was prohibited. He had taken a photo of the mayor's wife, of all people. That was abhorrent among Moslems. Ernie talked with the men, saying that the young man did not know their customs. He did not have any evil intentions. He had gotten lost on his way. He did not know the language. Paul, meanwhile, standing behind Ernie, was shrinking by the minute.

The police began their discussion all over again, saying that the man would have to hand over his camera. At that point, Ernie began executing all his persuasive powers to try to change their minds. He apologized profusely for the improper conduct of his copilot. He started telling them why they had come. Gradually, their faces became more friendly. Finally the mayor, who was also among them, demanded to be given the film. Paul did so, visibly relieved.

When the door was finally closed behind them, Ernie turned to his companion with a stern look.

"If it weren't so amusing, it would almost be sad. Do you know you could have landed in jail?"

In Tunis, their patience would be tested again. Of all days, they had arrived on the birthday of the prophet Mohammed. All the stores were closed. The whole city was celebrating. Did this mean Ernie and Paul would have to postpone continuing the trip? They hoped not!

The next leg of the journey was the long flight across the Mediterranean Sea. For safety reasons, they needed the rescue boat which had been sent to the Swiss Embassy. The next morning, the embassy staff received them in a friendly manner. To their utter disappointment, they found out that no rescue boat had arrived yet: the post office was still celebrating. How long would Mohammed's birthday last? Another day? Or two? Or three? As they kept inquiring, the ambassador himself caught wind of their dilemma. He greeted his fellow countrymen. He laughed about their problem and invited them to dinner. Surprised and grateful, they accepted his kind invitation.

What a pleasure to be able to taste a bit of home after all the complications! For Ernie, it seemed as though part of Switzerland had made its way across the waters to them. The tense and hectic journey was forgotten. Ernie began to relax as he shared his experiences.

"Are you not afraid of flying across the Mediterranean?" the ambassador wanted to find out.

"Well, I am no stranger to water," Ernie replied. "In my younger days, I worked on board a ship and crossed the Atlantic twenty-six times."

"Ever seasick?"

"No, never. The turbulence of the waves is just my kind of thing. Most of the passengers would stay in their cabins. A few courageous ones sat at the tables, so I'd tell them jokes while working to keep their minds off their problems."

"But how did you get started with your current work? The two don't seem to go together."

"The reason why I worked on those ships was because I wanted to go to America, 'the land of promise,' as they say. I wanted to emigrate and pursue my hobby–painting. I was hoping to meet some Americans who would want to support a poor Swiss artist. But that wasn't easy because almost everyone working on board that huge passenger steamer, the 'New Amsterdam,' had the same idea. Twice, a couple of Americans promised to put up $2,000 for me. The third American finally kept his promise. It was my reward for two years of hard labor on that ship. I didn't like the work, but I did achieve my goal. The day I went aboard as a passenger, I thought I had reached the end of the rainbow."

Ernie stopped for a minute. The ambassador listened in rapt attention.

"You've lived a very colorful life."

"But I was on the wrong track," Ernie continued. "I worked as a butler for my new boss. On the side, I attended an art school in Philadelphia. Everything was bigger, faster, higher, and more modern in the USA. Still, it didn't take long for me to see that the people were just the same as in Europe.

"While undergoing basic training at the Air Force in Texas, a military doctor found out I had tuberculosis. After spending a long time in hospital, I was honorably discharged. I returned to Philadelphia with one more disappointment to add to my collection. In my quest for purpose in life, I decided to change professions. I found an opening as a mechanic in training. I earned very little at that, so I began looking around for a profitable job on the side. I found a weekend job at a nightclub. It was near the highway on the way to the coast. I earned good money there.

"Sundays, I would go to church in that small town. One day the minister said we ought to keep the Sabbath holy and only do what was absolutely necessary. I knew my work was not in agreement with what the Bible said. Since I wanted to be a good citizen, I went to see my boss and quit. The last time I went to that small church, the pastor, standing at the exit, invited me over for dinner. He wanted to get to know me better. In answer to his questions, I first told him I'd been born in Switzerland, which I'd always been proud of. I shared that I had grown up in a religious family. I had been baptized and had even signed up for confirmation all on my own. I often prayed on good days and on bad. I spoke with such honest conviction that the pastor believed every word."

Ernie paused, thinking back. He had been so restless back then, without inner peace. He was so glad at the contentment he enjoyed these days—even if things didn't always work out perfectly.

"Let me finish answering your questions," he said to his host. "Going back to Philadelphia, on the way to work in the morning, I'd listen to the radio. A certain Pastor Palmer had a pretty famous radio program. His voice was calm and assuring. Somehow, what he was saying did something for me. One day he had a guest speaker on. I heard that he was going to speak at the Gospel Tabernacle that night. I liked his voice so I decided to go hear him there.

"Only a few people were in attendance. To stay on the safe side, I sat in the very back row below the balcony. The lights were not as bright there. I listened to the whole message. It was such a simple, modest man preaching such an impressive sermon! His words struck a deep chord in my heart. I could sense God wanted to talk to me. And I was ready to listen! I'll never forget that night. It must have been the most important one of my life. When the preacher asked if anyone had heard God's voice and wanted to respond, I jumped up. I thought this was my last chance. As I answered the invitation and walked down the aisle, I knew this was it–this was what I'd been looking for all of my life!

"You see," Ernie said turning to his host, "you need to evaluate how I got into my current occupation from that perspective. That night, I didn't just start a new life, but I also received a ministry. I attended a theological school for three years and studied the Bible. I returned to Switzerland wanting to tell Europeans that you could find everything you needed in America–even peace with God!"

"So, you regard your helicopter work as service to God?"

"Church services are only one part of it. As I understand the Bible, doing practical work and ministering to my fellow humans are just as important. Using the helicopter helps me combine both."

By the time Ernie and Paul said good-bye, they had forgotten all about Mohammed's birthday. The ambassador reminded them to pick up the emergency boat the next day. He shook their hands cordially, saying in closing, "Mr. Tanner, I'd like to wish you much success and say God bless you on all of your flights. How wonderful of Providence that we should meet!"

Chapter 23
The Pirate's Flight

Every year had its highlights. With time, you no longer saw the valleys you had to cross between mountain tops...they vanished into the foggy mist of memories. That's what would happen to Ernie and Hedi as they recollected the early years of the flying missions. The first few months of those years always belonged to Africa. For the Tanners, it meant separation and sacrifice. The remaining months of the year would run normally. Most of the time, it was not even apparent that this daddy was a pilot. Everybody simply had a job. Once in a while, they would talk about the Jet Ranger or the "old chopper," which was earning money in Greenland.

During vacation times, the family would enjoy camping. Sometimes a helicopter would fly along the coastline. Then everyone would stick their necks out of the tent to see where the sound was coming from. Flying did hold a fascination for them. They would discuss what model it had been, for example, Jet Ranger or Hughes.

As the end of the year drew near, however, and the children began looking forward to Christmas, Ernie's thoughts would race ahead into the new year. At night he would write down and organize his ideas. During the day, he'd put them into practice. Ethiopia was to be deluged with a massive aid campaign again the next year.

In November, Ernie started fundraising publicly. He was grateful to God that he had been able to gather the resources for another charter flight of supplies for Ethiopia. What he didn't know was what kind of a dangerous adventure he was placing himself into this time.

Through Mr. Aegerten of Air Transport Consultants, Ernie chartered a DC-7 from Air Management in Miami, Florida. He had had to make an advance payment of $20,000 for the flight from Zurich to Addis. Back then, that was quite a sum. Making preparations for this trip was intense. Contacting governmental and missions agencies in Ethiopia was time-consuming, not to mention obtaining the goods and choosing the team.

Finally, on January 16, 1975, everything was ready in Switzerland. Ernie Tanner, Werner Fuchs and Georg Ackermann formed the missions team, and Mr. Ueli Soltermann would join them as helicopter mechanic. He had taken a few days off and come to Kloten to dismantle the XCX; he would put it back together in Addis. Friends and acquaintances had also come to the airport to give them a helping hand. Then they wished them well and sent them on their way.

Ernie checked the supplies held in limbo in a large warehouse. The huge piles of flour sacks were quite a sight. They had been placed on seven low trolleys waiting in a long line. The Swiss Red Cross had donated twelve tons of a special kind of flour, consisting of wheat, soy and milk powder. The drilling device was loaded again, along with pipes and their respective pumps. Two Volkswagen engines and a couple of boxes with smaller items were sent along, too. The helicopter, of course, took up the most space.

Curious, Ernie stepped outside to see the DC-7.

"That must be it," he said to Georg, slightly disappointed, pointing to a large machine with four propellers. The fuselage was open, and a mechanic was working on an engine. Georg didn't know if he had enough guts to get into that old crate. A man in jeans walked up to Ernie, introducing himself as the pilot. The machine needed some work and would not be ready for takeoff for another two or three days. No need for discussion. Ernie knew he would simply have to accept the facts.

Two days later, loading all the supplies did not take long. The only question Ernie had was where he and the others were going to sit. There were three seats in the cockpit. He had four men, including himself, in his team. There were no other seats anywhere. At that time, Ernie began to worry. The cold January wind was already whistling through a bunch of cracks in the fuselage here on the ground. What were things going to be like up in the air?! What kind of company was Air Management, anyway? What about insurance for the passengers? The freight was insured but they were not. Of course, this wasn't considered a passenger flight!

"Mr. Joe, how long do you think it will take to make it to Addis?"

"Twelve to fourteen hours. Takeoff is tomorrow morning, okay?"

For Ernie, two important things remained to be done. He obtained life insurance policies for all four passengers–valid for two days. Afterward he drove home to get woolen blankets and sleeping bags so they wouldn't freeze to death onboard the DC-7.

January 20 came, and the DC-7 rolled onto the runway. Using every last ounce of thrust it had, the machine finally lifted off, barely managing the last few feet at the end of the runway. It was flying east at a low altitude across the Zurich area, which was covered in a blanket of snow.

Thank God, Hedi didn't know how much jeopardy her beloved husband would be in. This time, she would have had a real reason to worry. The first message she received came from Athens: the machine had had to land, due to "technical difficulties." As soon as the propellers came to a standstill, the burly mechanic got out his ladder and took a look at the engine. He loosened a part and let it fall to the ground with a bang. The four men, half-frozen, climbed out of their uncomfortable dungeon.

"When can we resume?"

"Midnight, at the earliest."

That was bad news. At least they could get something warm to eat at the airport. They comforted each other with stories of other adventures they had survived. In the face of them, their current situation was practically a cakewalk. Midnight came and went. The mechanic had a sour look on his face. He announced they would not get clearance before five o'clock in the morning. Whether they liked it or not, they would have to get out their sleeping bags and find a place to sleep in the airport hall. It wasn't very comfortable but at least it was safe.

During the next stage, they made it as far as Cairo after crossing the Mediterranean Sea in their wobbly DC-7. There, they had to get spare parts. It was probably going to take a couple of days. The "captain" advised his passengers to go find accommodations and then go see the Great Pyramids. Ernie agreed.

"Is everything included in the price on this trip?" he quipped.

The American mechanic just shook his head sympathetically. Still, Ernie did not give up hope of arriving in Addis eventually.

On the third day, the machine was "all right" again. Ernie looked for a spot to sit down between various boxes and bags, praying for the situation. Everyone looked a tad concerned as the "crate" finally made it into the air. It seemed to be spitting fire and was making a deafening noise. Ernie looked out the window at the wing with its two propellers. Then he looked down at the desert. He thanked God for the assurance of being safe in his heavenly Father's care. He sat there, lost in thought for a long time, listening to the sound of the engine. Then he remembered the life insurance policies: they were no longer valid. Now their safety lay completely in the hands of the One over them all.

A change in the background noise sent a chill down Ernie's spine. Was he mistaken or had they landed already? The propeller spun to a stop. He stood up nervously and made his way to the cockpit.

"What's going on?" he asked, pointing to the engine which was finally not making a sound.

"Well, we had to land in Djibouti", the pilot said, calm as could be. "We won't make it up to Addis with only three engines," he said, turning to look out the window.

Ernie had had enough. Despite the protests of the pilot, the helicopter was unloaded then and there. Ueli Soltermann assembled it in record time. He was in a hurry himself because he had been expected back at work in Switzerland days ago. He caught a Swissair flight ready for takeoff at the last minute.

Georg Ackermann volunteered to stay with the DC-7 to watch the freight. Ernie and Werner started the ignition of the helicopter to fly out to Addis. This time they felt safe. The next day, Georg also landed in Addis with the DC-7. He approached his friends, telling them breathlessly that, back in Djibouti, they had had to turn around again since one of the jet's engines had caught on fire. It had taken even more repair work before they could leave for Addis. Their clever mechanic had made a mistake by mounting the exhaust backwards.

The first letter which Hedi received from Addis began, "Now, the flight at the hands of that pirate is over..."

Chapter 24

Emergency Landing

Ernie had not forgotten about those tribes the missionary had spoken of. He had a destination in mind in the southern part of the country, the Gemu-Gofa Province. Upon arrival, he made acquaintance with the Bodi tribe, who had a reputation for being naked, wild murderers. The Quegu tribe also lived in the region— fearful nomads who were often suppressed by the Bodi. Then he encountered the tribe of the Mursi. Their women, with distended lips, have an unusual appearance. In a ritual act, their lower lips are slit open on the side to make room for a spherical plate of clay.

The chopper helped bring the message of Christ's love to all of these tribes. In addition, a few Europeans were also to come in contact with the Good News. Ernie did his best to leave no one out. Two Swedish men, Count Carl Gustav von Rosen and his son Eric, were working for an Ethiopian disaster relief agency. Using Saab airplanes, they dropped off "food bombs" by flying at lower altitudes. One of these machines with Eric as its pilot crashed up in the mountains. Ernie flew the three injured crew members to the hospital in Arba Minch. Among those men was a well-known Swedish journalist. He wrote an article about the rescue:

> ...we were flying medicine into an epidemic area of Ethiopia. One native was accompanying us. After we'd been in the air about thirty minutes, we encountered extreme downwash which caused us to crash into a river valley. It was a miracle we survived: our plane was a total wreck. It had done a somersault. We landed in a bush, luckily, which softened the impact a little. We sustained serious back injuries and concussions. Our faces were cut up a great deal. Thanks to inhabitants of the valley

who'd made a great rescue effort, we were able to reach a nearby village. It took three hours. The plane's radio was of no use in that area.

Two village boys, however, offered to walk to the nearest town although it would take eight hours. From there, a Norwegian missionary informed Eric's father, Carl Gustav von Rosen, of what had happened. He himself is a pilot. He was able to contact Ernie Tanner the following morning. Von Rosen flew his plane, and Ernie Tanner, his helicopter. Both arrived in the skies above the village simultaneously at noon. While von Rosen couldn't land his machine, it was no problem for Tanner. He was able to set down nearly next to us. What an experience for us! We'd already been waiting a whole day. I had almost given up all hope that help would come. I'd remembered that Ernie Tanner, whom I had met before, had told me he would be leaving the area. Fortunately, he hadn't yet.

I don't dare to think of what would have happened had Tanner not come to our rescue with his helicopter. We had such severe injuries that we were unable to walk or ride on a mule. I knew we needed medical attention as quickly as possible. There was no one in the village able to help clean our dirty wounds. I seriously doubt that we would have lived if it hadn't been for his help. It took only thirty minutes for him to get us to the Norwegian mission hospital. There, we received the best of medical treatment.

I'm persuaded that thousands of people in that impassible mountainous area are being greatly helped through the selfless work of Helimission. The task is enormous! I believe the people who support the mission should receive the whole picture of the significance of Ernie Tanner's work down there. For this reason, Eric von Rosen and I would like to thank those standing behind Helimission from the bottom of our hearts for their support.

Lars Braw,
Editor in Chief of the Swedish Newspaper
Kvällposten

The second significant event of that year was not a highlight but a low point: an emergency landing due to engine trouble. Ernie was in the air with an Ethiopian governor when a turbine suddenly failed. Immediately he set the chopper on autorotation, looking for a possible spot to land. Quickly, he decelerated past some skinny cows and landed the machine roughly but still under control on a soft hill in a meadow. One skid sunk into the ground on the side of the hill. The other one on the opposite side stood stuck in a large anthill which kept the machine from toppling over. The men got out unharmed.

When Ernie told the puzzled governor what had happened, he embraced Ernie, repeating, "God has saved our lives, you great man!"

Misfortune had come quickly, but recovering from its effects would take a long time. Fortunately the Ethiopian official was with him. He marched into the next village and notified the police. Then he organized a watchman for the helicopter and informed missions headquarters of the accident.

When the sobering news reached Hedi in Trogen, she wrote about it to all their friends and supporters in Switzerland:

On February 24, the time of mobility Ernie has enjoyed with the helicopter came to an unfortunate end. Both passengers were able to leave the machine uninjured after an emergency landing. It has not, however, been possible to get the chopper started again. A Heliswiss mechanic has flown to Ethiopia. It seems to be a complex issue. Hopefully, I'll be able to send you a more positive report soon.

At the bottom of her letter, she added the following:

> I have just learned that large components of the helicopter have been removed and sent to Switzerland for inspection. This will take about one month. Ernie will, therefore, be coming back home in a couple of days. This is bad news, and yet, good!

Ernie stood in front of the helicopter, unable to say a word. He simply could not understand why it wouldn't fly any more. Why on earth had the turbine failed...why... in this remote, rugged, deserted area? The turbine–this meant the heart of the machine was beating no more. How was he going to get it out of this place? How far was it to the next road? He sat down in the shade of the machine and prayed.

A long procedure was to follow. Back in the capital city, Ernie contacted Heliswiss in Switzerland. They wanted to send a mechanic to check out the helicopter. Ernie and the mechanic left Addis by car and had to continue on foot. Now it was time to do some hard work in the scorching African heat. The turbine was removed, along with the tail. Through the impact of the landing, it had been dented. Several other parts were also dismantled and placed in boxes. Many indigenous helpers came to assist. They helped carry loads to the road. Then, everything was shipped from Addis Ababa to Switzerland.

Ernie returned home as well–tired, exhausted and ill. He had barely begun to relax and enjoy his children's spring break with them when the next blow came.

On Easter Monday, Hedi received a strange phone call which she did not quite understand. Ernie was not at home. A woman was on the line, saying a helicopter was on its way from Basle to Bern. She gave Hedi evasive answers to her concerned questions. She kept repeating that there was a lot of snow in the Jura Mountains, and the helicopter could not get any further. She said it was possible that something awful had happened. When Hedi asked about the pilot, she was told he would contact her himself.

Confused and shocked, Hedi sat by the phone. What had happened? What did the woman have to do with the whirlybird? Was it their old XDK? It had been located in Basle—that was true. They had rented it to someone, so that was accurate as well. Why did the pilot not call himself? Why had this strange, nervous-sounding woman been on the line? And why did she seem so shaken?

All the questions were resolved that same night. In bad weather, the XDK had been flown from Basle across the Jura Mountains. It could not manage a certain altitude with three passengers on board, so landing had been necessary. Two people got off. When the pilot tried to start the machine again, the XDK turned over and caught fire. Both crew members had been able to jump out, which spared their lives. This was what Hedi was told about the situation.

An enormous pressure settled on her chest.

"If only Ernie were here! I can't take this by myself," she cried. "Our old 'J'!"

It had been their very first machine. To them it was symbolic of overcoming a very hard start. Ernie and Hedi had invested their everything into it. A new phase in the history of missions had been launched with it. Now, it was gone. Hedi could hardly believe it.

"The vision has to be tried in fire," Ernie said when he heard the bad news.

One helicopter had been destroyed, and the second one badly needed repairs. It seemed as if the validity of Helimission itself was being questioned. Had God withdrawn His blessing?

Part Four

Chapter 25

Freeing Hostages in Bulki

Despite all the setbacks, Ernie's heart was still on fire for relief work in Ethiopia. April 19th was the target date to resume. He had gotten rested since the last mission. When the time came to leave his "home, sweet home" in Trogen, he was full of energy and encouraged in his faith.

He and two mechanics flew to Addis with Ethiopian Airlines, taking a new turbine and various boxes with them. A truck transported all of the material from Bulki, a small airport in the southern area of the country, close to where the helicopter was waiting. From there, Africans managed the last leg on foot, carrying heavy loads over to Charlie. Hedi, knowing this in advance, had sent along summer dresses and sweaters collected from Swiss friends. She wanted to send a token of her gratitude for their enormous service of love. A few days later, Charlie was in the air again. While the checks and repairs had been taken care of, Georg had stayed in Ethiopia, working at a mission's headquarters. Now Ernie's faithful friend was back, prepared to once again go through thick and thin with them.

There was a mission station in Bulki with a small runway which had just been finished. Under a Communistic regime, however, missions work was getting more and more difficult. People were afraid of losing their jobs if the missionaries, teachers and nurses would leave the premises. In two cases, the employees locked up their own missionaries to prevent them from exiting the country. One of these incidents involved the Ratslif family. The situation was so serious that Brother Ratslif suffered two heart attacks in a row. He desperately needed medical attention. A teacher from Bulki, an Ethiopian, did not allow him to leave the house.

The government, meanwhile, did not permit him to be picked up by plane.

Ernie learned of the emergency and called General Mobratu in Addis Ababa. Mobratu, governor of the Gemu-Gofa Province, was a short, friendly Ethiopian and was greatly respected in Arba Minch. Ernie's headquarters were also in Arba Minch, so they knew each other very well. You could say they had become friends. The governor promised to help with the tenuous situation in Bulki. He called back a short while later.

"Mr. Tanner, take the police chief of Arba Minch with you and pick up the police chief of Felega Naway," he instructed. "Then, fly out to Bulki and take Mr. and Mrs. Ratslif to the hospital today! I have instructed both men accordingly."

The policeman from Arba Minch, a strong, tall man, found his way to the heliport in no time at all. In Felega Naway, the second man joined them in the chopper. Ernie flew along the steep incline of the mountains. This range separated the Omo Valley from the rest of the world. When landing in Bulki, Ernie always had to compete with the wind. To the left of the landing strip, there were the four buildings from the mission. To the right, there was a slope where the village was located. Ernie got down closer, seeing only a couple of children. Then he spotted adults walking up the path, carrying rifles. The atmosphere was charged. As the turbine cooled down, the people walked toward them, reaching the edge of the airstrip. Breathing heavily, they encircled the helicopter.

Ernie would never forget the look of shock on the people's faces as the two policemen got out of the helicopter. They stood like frozen statues in front of the crowd. No one dared to make a move. Finally, the police ordered everyone to sit down. The children and dogs were sent away. Then someone was told to bring Brother Ratslif over. He came, though having to make a great effort. As soon as he laid eyes on Ernie, his face lit up in surprise. The two greeted each other.

Only now did the police allow one of the village elders to offer an explanation. He brought ridiculous accusations against this faithful, aging missionary. Ratslif was then allowed to speak.

"Working side by side with you, I've built a school and a road, partly with my own hands. My home was open to every one of you at all times. Now, you are treating me like some criminal because I want to leave...because I have to leave. I've had two heart attacks. And this is truly breaking my heart."

He broke down in tears. Everyone was quiet. Now it was Ernie's turn to talk.

"I've been commanded by General Mobratu to fly Mr. Ratslif to the hospital. It's almost five o'clock now. I would like to ask Mr. Ratslif to get his things together."

"I've been ready for two weeks!" he cried. His wife brought over two suitcases immediately. The chopper was loaded up in an instant. Ernie was glad to take off, leaving a surprised crowd behind them. Yet, did they know what they had just lost, he thought to himself? A father. A friend. A counselor. A helper. It was too late now. For years to come, no other helicopter and no other missionary would come to Bulki.

Chapter 26

Four Mysterious Letters

The mailman often brought bundles of mail addressed to "House Salem." This time, however, he brought four blue aerograms which Hedi spotted instantly. Her heart began beating faster in anticipation. Quickly, she pulled the first one from the pile. Yes, it was Ernie's handwriting. There was a big "3" written on it. What was that supposed to mean? There was a "2" on another one. But number "1" was missing! Hedi found it, along with number "4" as well. She sat down at the kitchen table. Everything else was irrelevant now. Letters–how easily they could have gotten lost, stolen or been sabotaged by strikes! This time, they had come through. They had traveled from Ethiopia to Switzerland; that is, from the desert...the jungle...the mountains of Africa...all the way to the peaceful hills of the Appenzellerland.

Carefully, Hedi opened the first letter with a kitchen knife.

"My darling wife..." it began.

Her heart was pounding even harder. A flood of tender, loving emotions overtook her. Her hands trembled as she read Ernie's handwriting. It was not as generous as usual. The lines were squeezed onto the page:

How are you? I am hoping that, for once, you will get this letter quickly. I am sitting out here in the bush on a lonely plateau in the middle of a deserted airstrip. Maybe it belonged to an oil company once. There is no hut or any other kind of accommodation nearby. I had to land because I ran out of fuel. Georg and I had been preparing to fly from Addis to Cameroon when the government asked me to make a relief flight. About one hundred and fifty students are supposed to have been cut off from the rest of the country as a result of the river flooding over.

The flood area is in Ogaden in far-east Ethiopia, far away from Arba Minch. I didn't have an adequate flight chart of Ogaden. Everything had already been packed in Addis, and I was wondering whether I should do the trip anyway. Then, I agreed. Georg helped me to put in the spare fuel can. We filled her up and took off. I had a Michelin chart and could at least identify some rivers and a place called Kelafo. That was our destination. Due to a faulty fuel gauge, we had only filled up the tank halfway. I didn't realize it until we had been in the air for over half-an-hour. We would've had enough juice, had I found Kelafo fast enough.

We had already flown four hours and should have been arriving in the flood region surrounding the Skibeli River. The water was glistening below us in the evening sun. We were quite happy as we began our descent between pillars of clouds. There was all this water in the middle of nowhere– after 375 miles of desert! I landed near some huts and asked where Kelafo was. Some sad-looking persons pointed upstream. What a terrible sight! There were dead, stinking animal carcasses all over. In the last moments of daylight, we took off one more time with only a few gallons of fuel left. As we flew back, we saw the extent of the flood. For miles, there was only water–water and sandbanks and bushes. It was impossible to tell where the original riverbed had been.

The letter was over. Hastily, Hedi opened the second one and read on:

To the north of the river, the area plateaued off. There, I saw a large airstrip. This could be Gode, I thought. On my chart, I had seen a military airfield in Gode. They must have fuel here! But our hopes were soon dashed. Upon flying over it, I saw that it was deserted. Heavy-hearted, I decided to land, nonetheless. Immediately, I set off a flare, hoping that someone in Gode would see it. Just before it got totally dark, we gathered some wood to make a fire to keep predators at bay.

After an uncomfortable night, we tried to reach Kelafo on foot very early the next morning. I locked up the helicopter carefully and asked God to protect it. We tried to get our bearings, looking down into that wide river area with washed out, unidentifiable banks. We marched along a road going upstream. At various ponds, we stopped to filter and drink some water, filling our canisters as well. It was terribly hot. We wrapped our pajamas around our heads. After walking a long time, we came to a vast plain without even one tree or shrub. We only had two pints of water left. What were we supposed to do? Continue or go back? The decision was hard. We decided to return. That saved us.

Near the river, we saw some huts. Georg waded through knee-deep water, returning with two other men. It was already 5:30 p.m. We asked the two men to take a message to Kelafo, and I offered them eight dollars. They wanted sixteen. What choice did I have? So, I paid them. One of them remembered he was sick and needed medicine which also cost eight dollars, so I gave it to him. We said good-bye, emphasizing once again how important it was for them to go there.

Then, we sought the way back to the helicopter. It was already dark. Eerie sounds in the wilderness were not lost on our ears. Both of us were exhausted and discouraged. We had reached the end of our rope. Unsure of whether we were still on the right track, we, after what seemed like ages, found ourselves at our starting point on the plateau again. In the moonlight, we saw our helicopter waiting for us.

Hedi let out a long sigh. Then, she tore open number "3." To just sit there, not being able to help, was hard. Would this letter have a better ending?

As I turned the lock on the helicopter door, I was in for a terrible shock. The window had been broken. Someone had tried to open it by force. The place where the window had been damaged was exactly where I had placed my hand in the morning. I had "laid hands" on it as I prayed and asked God for His safe keeping. Thank God, He had heard us! Otherwise, the strangers would have plundered our bird and made off with our precious water supply! Another night in the chopper. It was not very comforting to know other people in the vicinity could be watching us. We remained on our guard. I slept inside of the helicopter; Georg, underneath it. We set an alarm clock to go off every hour. Then, we would put more wood on the fire and change positions.

At the break of dawn, we began to crane our necks, expecting help to come. If those men had left the previous night–or so we thought–they could be back around midday. Around 10:30 a.m., three people appeared at the edge of the field. It was our "friends" from the day before. They had brought a third friend who also wanted eight dollars to go to Kelafo. Instead of taking four hours to walk to Kelafo, they had taken two hours to hike from their hut to the helicopter, in order to ask for another eight dollars. To be on the safe side, we decided that Georg was to go with them this time. They walked away in a leisurely manner, leaving me behind– waiting quite anxiously. All kinds of thoughts come to you at such times. I had a really hard time to keep from worrying, I tell you.

In the afternoon, two men approached from another direction to "visit." They were thirsty and asked for water. I gave them a cup from my precious supply, indicating that they would have to share it. The first one gulped it down all by himself and held out the cup again. I sacrificed a second one. They also wanted clothing and whatever else I could spare. Without a thank-you or good-bye, they left. I watched them go, glad to be alone once again.

"This story is really long," Hedi groaned. "Number '4' will surely bring a happy end," she thought, hoping for the best before continuing to read.

My dinner was a cup of water and half-a-cup of oatmeal. I fell asleep without tending to the fire. I was simply too tired. At 10 p.m., I had a rude awakening—a lion was roaring nearby. Half an hour later, I woke up again. This time, a man's voice had startled me. I saw three men coming closer, lamp in hand, crossing the large field. One of them was holding up something shiny and red. As they got nearer, I recognized it as a thermos bottle. Were they the three guys from this morning? No, they were three strangers who offered me hot tea. What did they want at this time of night? I remembered the broken window. Had these tall Somalis tried to get into the chopper? Was I to give them what they wanted under any circumstance?

Very skeptically, I sat down with them in the dirt and drank of their hot, strong tea. One of them got up and studied the helicopter with interest, rubbing across it with his hands. I told him to get them off it. He examined the lock and then opened the door. I got up and closed it again. Then, the fellow started getting angry, waving his hands about and threatening me.

I was startled. So this was their intention—getting me into an argument. I went from being fearful to being incensed. I remained firm and tried to calm the man down. He kept getting angrier. Then, I had a feeling something was happening behind me. I turned around. The other two had stood up, pulling rifles out of their long cloaks.

The letter had ended with Ernie's handwriting becoming tinier and tinier. But where was number "5"?! And the happy end? Hedi turned the letter around, looking for a continuation. There was nothing but the address and the large "4."

Her initial joy over those letters gave way to frantic questions.

"But, of course," Hedi comforted herself, "these letters must have gotten to the post office somehow. My dearest Ernie must have found some way out of that terrible mess."

She folded the letters back up and tried to go back to business.

As it turned out, Georg and those three men had reached the mission headquarters in Kelafo after a long, tiresome march. They spent the night there. The next day, he, another missionary and four natives drove back to the deserted airfield in a Land Rover. They saw the helicopter from a distance. Next to it was the reserve tank upon which sat an interesting rocket-like object. Ernie stood up and let out a joyful yell as he saw the vehicle speeding toward him. It left a huge dusty cloud in its wake.

Ernie was so moved at help's arrival that he could hardly talk. Together, they thanked God for His help in time of need. Then Ernie told them what had happened the previous night.

"As soon as I saw the rifles," he began, "my arms shot up in the air. I cried out loud for God to help me. Then, I suddenly remembered the two flares in my shirt pocket. I pulled them out and put one in each hand. I pointed them at the crooks and screamed at the top of my lungs, 'Get out of here!' Shaken, they took a step back. They probably doubted the genuineness of my weapons.

One of them then picked up a rock to throw at my head. Then I pulled the trigger, pointing it right above his head. He dropped it, backing off a little. I cried out again for God to help me and save my life. Tired and trembling with fear, I pointed my flare gun toward them. One of the flares had already been used up; I would have been lost, had they known. Walking backwards, they seemed to be withdrawing. Then, one grabbed the thermos, moving fast as a cat. The second one picked up rocks and starting throwing them at me. I heard them passing right by my head. One of them hit a window of the helicopter."

Remembering this terrifying incident, Ernie became worked up all over again.

"They remained standing at a distance, so I got out my camera and began flashing at them. They finally left."

Georg had a question, "What is the meaning of this little apparatus right here?"

He pointed to the "weapon" on top of the spare can and smiled.

"Well, those are my two last big flares—just in case."

The following day, the long-awaited hum of an approaching engine sounded in the sky. An airplane touched down. Soon, the helicopter was tanked up and ready to go again.

Ernie was glad to leave this land of lions, vultures and other predators behind him. However, he considered himself all the richer for, once again, having experienced God's goodness and faithfulness firsthand.

Chapter 27

Expand...But How?

Ernie Tanner had entitled his venture "Helimission." In 1974 it had become a foundation with statutes and a board of directors. At the beginning, the mission only had the one helicopter, of course, "J," which Ernie could fly himself. He used the machine to serve missionaries during the dry season in Africa. Meanwhile, Ernie stayed busy the rest of the year, raising finances in Switzerland with his documentaries. Problems stayed at a minimum.

With the expansion of their "fleet" from one to two machines, however, things began to get unexpectedly complicated. The most difficult part was finding personnel. Helicopter pilots were few and far between in Switzerland. It was not exactly a piece of cake to find the right person. Many were quick to say that missions work, not flying, was their highest goal in life. In actuality, they just wanted to get an exciting job in Africa. Then, they would discover what it meant being cut off from all the amenities and all they held dear in Europe. The pilots would have to deal with unpleasant organizational tasks and also cope with technical setbacks. These pressures certainly brought to the surface what stuff they were made of—and who was for real. You could tell who was sincere: they were the ones who turned to the Source of all life for their strength during those trips.

Ernie returned to Cameroon in early 1976. This time he flew a Cessna 320, a twin-engine machine. He was joined by a certain Mr. Henseler, who was organizing an air rally. Even then, Ernie was secretly dreaming of a second helicopter to be able to serve both the eastern and western coasts simultaneously. He was on the lookout for a new pilot and also needed some new equipment for the chopper. Both were problematic. Obtaining the necessary hardware seemed easier. After all, with a little research you can pretty much narrow down what you need, inform yourself about the best options, find out what is technically leading the market, and so on. There is less risk.

On the "software" side, you can request a list of references for a pilot, but you can never totally see into his or her heart. You can ascertain a person's skills, ask for a short resume, even inquire about his faith walk. However, in contrast to a machine, you cannot predict how he or she will react in critical situations. All the "knowns and unknowns" kept Ernie dependent upon God. He went to prayer, asking the Lord for wisdom and strength in making decisions.

The mission to Cameroon took place from mid-January through mid-March. It was a total success once again. Heliswiss was in charge of the technical maintenance, even a continent away. Two of their mechanics flew to Cameroon when a comprehensive check and some modifications were required. They labored in the hot tropical sun of Yaounde for eleven days. The new blades they mounted on the main rotor cost 40,000 Swiss-Francs alone. In addition, they installed a particle separator to keep whirling sand out of the turbine. They also built in an HF radio and did a thorough job of carrying out the mandatory inspection after every 300 flight hours.

As soon as Charlie was ready for takeoff again, Ernie and Georg started on their journey across Africa. They were no first-timers to the route and reached Addis Ababa without problem on March 20th. Georg was happy to stay in Ethiopia to work for the Red Sea Mission Team. Ernie, however, was longing for home with every fiber of his being. Important appointments had been taken care of. Now the most important for him was being with his family. What a joy to come home during spring break—when the kids were off! The Tanner children were waiting for him at their favorite gathering place, a sunny spot near a stream in the woods. There, they had plenty of peace and quiet. There was also plenty of room for exploring, climbing, building, playing, singing–or simply doing nothing.

Chapter 28
"Dearest Hedi..."

In this day and age of e-mail, it is hard to remember how valuable a letter once was–and can still be today. Letters are a wonderful means of communication. You can read them over and over again without having to fire up a computer. Unlike electronic mail, you can hold one in your hands. Letters have a certain "mystery" to them. They build bridges across oceans and across continents. Nothing can convey the emotions of the writer better than a "love letter." Some letters are so precious they are saved in wooden chests for a lifetime. Letters can, however, also cause yearning and pain.

Ernie and Hedi were diligent correspondents. Between January and March during the Cameroon mission, Hedi wrote twenty-four letters. During his mission to Ethiopia from April until June, Ernie wrote twelve. There was so much to ask...to share...to explain... to whisper. This was not the age of international calls, cell phones, faxes or e-mails. Telegrams would often get lost. It was, therefore, the season of writing letters. The letters helped build a solid bridge between Africa and Switzerland. Through them, Hedi received a pretty clear picture of the many fine details that made up Ernie's days. Whether the experiences were good or bad, they could be summed up in one word: Africa.

Addis
April 23, 1976

I sat next to the head of a Danish mission on the plane. I had met him in Copenhagen years ago. He told me that they have an urgent need of a helicopter to transport supplies for a hospital. Tomorrow, Georg and I will travel to Awaza, along with members of the World Health Organization

(WHO). On Monday, I will leave there to fly to Kelafo. The entire valley is flooded. About 600,000 people have been affected. A chopper from an organization that gives vaccinations for smallpox is scouting out the area. We will immediately start our effort by supplying the people with food and vaccine as well.

At the same time, I am about to buy a second-hand Land Rover, a 1972 model with twelve seats and 50,000 miles on it, for $13,000. It belongs to the UN, making it exempt from customs and taxes. I still need the approval of the Ethiopian Development Aid Committee so that I can purchase the vehicle under those same conditions. In exchange, they want to hold the deed: I still have to talk them out of that! Starting Monday, we will be camping out, living in a tent and cooking over a fire. Our comfort is that we are bringing help to thousands and are saving lives. I will do my best that the people won't just "see" the Gospel but also "hear" it.

Awaza,
April 25, 1976

After a long, bumpy ride, we've made it to Awaza. We're staying directly on a lake with a family from the smallpox relief effort. Tomorrow, I'm to fly the husband to El Kere. The missionaries in Dollo don't have any more food, so we'll bring them staples tomorrow. We just took a test flight, and everything is in perfect order. Tomorrow, Dr. Weithaler will come with us to Dollo. In the evening, he's promised to take this letter with him to Addis.

In the meantime, I've been swimming in this wonderful lake. There are no Bilharzia parasites or crocodiles here, only hippos, and they're my friends anyway. I wonder what you're doing at this moment. Maybe you're at our favorite spot by the stream. My thoughts are scurrying across the desert and across the Mediterranean to all of you in my beloved Salem. I trust that Immanuel's job training is going well. I hope Lucky is having fun in kindergarten and that everyone else is doing well at school, too....

April 26, 1976

Just a few thoughts in a hurry while I'm eating. Our stuff hasn't come yet. I've bought the Land Rover. We've received a landing permit for a whole year. We are sending the milk powder directly to SIM in Addis. They're going to distribute it in the Puch camp. When "Werni" comes, please have him bring some cheese for fondue!

Awaza
April 29, 1976

So much has happened since my last letter. On Monday, Karl Mueller, with whom we are staying here, Dr. Weithaler, as well as a Swedish missionary and I took 220 lbs. of food supplies to Dollo. It is located at the border of Kenya and Somalia. We had wanted to take Mr. Mueller to El Kere, which lies on the other side of the Bale Mountains. At 14,100 ft. above sea-level, those mountains were way up in the clouds. I flew up to 13,000 ft., which took a lot of fuel.

The men said they knew the area well, and I took their word for it. When we came down out of the clouds, they had no clue as to where we were. It is hard to know because the desert begins there. There are no villages, roads or rivers as landmarks to keep you from losing your orientation. To stay on schedule, we needed to find El Kere and land there. We flew around for a long time and used up our fuel. I finally saw a river and a place to land on an open field. There was not a soul to be found anywhere! Mr. Mueller had a tent with room for two with him. The Swede and I slept in the chopper. Then, we built an airstrip 650 ft. in length. We didn't have to worry about hunger; we had 220 lbs. of food with us! We also hunted down an animal somewhat smaller than a gazelle.

On Wednesday morning, I used my VHF radio to contact another aircraft we heard buzzing over us. We gave them our position, and two hours later Eric von Rosen was circling over us. He flew all the way down from Makale to get us. Shortly after that, another machine flew by as well, and then a "Smallpox Aid" machine brought us fuel. What a feeling! As Eric was getting closer, Dr. Weithaler began praising God out loud with "Hallelujah!" and "Amen!" It was a hard but good experience. Vultures were close by, but our Savior was even closer!

I only made one flight over to El Kere yesterday. Eric gave me a big hug there. Then I took the food over to Dollo. This morning, it was "back to Awaza." Now at 2 p.m., I am off to Kelafo where people are anxiously awaiting us. That is why this hello is so short. Have "Werni" bring us some more flares. They're in my office on the floor behind the door. Please say thank you very much to all our intercessors.

The Desert
May 4, 1976

I'm writing to you from the border directly between Ethiopia and Somalia. This morning, I took the police chief, an administrator and two other "big shots" to a meeting with some Somali officers. I didn't know what it was all about and emphatically refused to fly all the way to the border. They just told me they had to do a border control along that route. Finally, I agreed to fly them about three miles outside of the border area. We landed on an airstrip which was being closely guarded. I immediately saw that the military had been informed of our coming via radio. We drove up to the border in a truck and were escorted to some tents where the Somalian "higher-ups" welcomed us. We were seated at a long table and were served drinks by some ladies who were all dressed up for the occasion. Only then was I informed that we were meeting with "neighbors."

The atmosphere is amiable: they even appear happy that I am there. Now, they are all giving their speeches. I don't understand a word, so I am using the time to drop you a few lines. The surroundings are very impressive. I'm the only Caucasian here among all of these important officials. Our table gives us a view of a vast plain with some mountains in the distance. If any journalists could see me, they'd be jealous, for sure.

The last couple of days, we've been busy with smallpox flights. Whenever I would find myself waiting for the medical teams, I'd put on an audiotape where Scriptures were being read in the Somali language. Everywhere I went, the listeners seemed grateful.

The situation at the Kelafo headquarters is still critical. Despite all the muck and mire, the helpers are able to treat the sick and bring children into the world. Everyone is sweating up a storm! Things will be better there in a couple of weeks' time. In the meantime, we've been able to fix up a Toyota Jeep and a Land Rover. We used them to repair the airstrip so that smaller planes can land again. Then they won't be limited to using helicopters anymore. Georg and I have both had quite a bit of stomach trouble. Thankfully, things have gotten better in that department.

Arba Minch,
May 5, 1976

We didn't return from the border until 3 p.m., and then I delivered supplies from the airport to Kelafo until 6:45 p.m. It went very well and very fast. The entire city was watching since they'd never seen our kind of external transports before.

Last night, the river suddenly rose to twelve inches below the dam. While it was still dark, I moved the helicopter to a safer place. The headquarters had to be evacuated. We spent the night on higher ground, out in the open under the stars. Although we had cots to sleep on, I didn't get much shut-eye. The mosquitoes were torture.

Once again, a day is coming to a close. To me, it feels like it's been a week.

Arba Minch,
May 26, 1976

Bark Fahnestock and I went on a scouting expedition over to the tribes living on the Omo River. We managed to shoot two buffalo. We gave them to the Mursi to eat, for they had been going without food for a while. Three native evangelists who went hunting with us gained great respect from the Mursi. We couldn't have done them a bigger favor. They carried every bit of the animals home. They even make shoes out of the skins, which are about an inch thick. We also encountered a small tribe, called the Quegu. We stayed overnight with them, and they honored us by slaughtering a goat. They had never heard of the name of Jesus.

This week was very busy. Ethiopian Airlines didn't fly the entire time because they don't have enough aircrafts. So everyone wanted my services. Before long, a Jumbo Jet will be too small to hold them all!

Chapter 29
The Flight Rally

Wolf Weinlechner was a good friend, and our relationship to one another would soon bear more fruit. Wolf's boss, who was always concerned about safety, decided to sell his twin-engine helicopter. He decided to switch to a German BO 105. The machine, carefully developed and built in Munich, had a reliable reputation. Ernie learned from Wolf that his boss was looking for a buyer for the Jet Ranger. The exterior of this Ranger looked just like Charlie's. It was several years younger, though, and had a more powerful turbine. Furthermore, it had an additional fuel tank, landing gear with automatically inflatable floating devices and many other good features–plus, it was in top condition.

On April 30, Ernie was able to purchase the orange Jet Ranger for $105,000, that is, 264,239.50 Swiss-Francs, in cash. To him, it was a miracle. He was so thankful for the dear friends, supporters and intercessors who stood so faithfully by his side, making this possible. At the same time, it gave him a boost to keep pursuing the unusual path he had chosen.

The new helicopter was given the name HB-XDY, "D" for Delta and "Y" for Yankee. It was to stay in Cameroon, West Africa, permanently. Charlie, then, would be on call in Eastern Africa for both Kenya and Ethiopia. Ernie already had a young Swiss pilot named Werni in mind to fly Charlie. It was he whom Ernie had been expecting so eagerly in Arba Minch. For the "Yankee," a Swede was in the running. He had to pass a two-month trial period in 1977 in Cameroon. At the end of the year, Ernie contacted Mr. Henseler again. An air rally was scheduled for the beginning of the year. A film producer was interested in that. Not only did he want to film the rally but he also planned to take shots of Ernie Tanner and Helimission in action. Before the year was over, a film team showed up in Trogen.

"Good Morning, Mr. Tanner. Nice to meet you in person," the producer began. "May I introduce my co-worker, Gernod?"

Gernod was a tall, friendly German. He carried a film camera, an audio recorder and several lights around with him.

"Pleased to meet you, Mr. Tanner. Sorry for all the inconvenience, but we wouldn't get very far without the equipment," Gernod apologized.

Ernie turned to the producer, "Mr. Toegel, please make yourself at home. This is our little office. Just put your stuff down on the floor there. Yes, that would be fine."

"In order to not waste any time, why don't we have some statements right away," Toegel suggested.

Slightly surprised, Ernie looked at the two men who quickly set up their lights and got everything ready to start recording.

"Wow, you've got a wonderful map of Africa right here," the producer said, pointing to the wall. "In a minute, you're going to show us the route and explain a few things to us. Just act as if you are talking to your wife. Oh, yes, Mrs. Tanner, there you are. You don't need to be nervous. You don't have to say a single word. You just stand there, listening to your husband. Try to act interested. Okay, let's try it."

Mr. Toegel, a young, accomplished film professional in faded jeans and a red sweater, knew just how to set them at ease.

"And the children? They'll be back home from school soon, right? Very good! Those shots are going to be just great."

Mr. Toegel had a new idea.

"We'll have the family on an outing, wading through the snow while their father sweats in the heat of Africa.

And now, it's your turn, Mr. Tanner. Have you given your role some thought?"

Ernie laughed. He wasn't as confident as Mr. Toegel but nodded anyhow, turning toward the map.

A short while later, the first couple of children peeped through the door. A bit nervous but more curious, they all came inside, admiring the large spotlights. They watched the two men at work, making mysterious gestures, intently. Their strict father, however, was not putting up with the distraction.

Pointing to the door, he said sternly, "Go back to the house and wait there until we come over. Then it'll be your turn."

About half an hour later, the three of them lugged the entire equipment over to the house, just clearing the low doorframe. The kids had, in the meantime, busied themselves with other things. The oldest was playing piano. The girls had spread out their stamps on the large kitchen table, sorting them out by country. The youngest, Lucky, was setting up a crane and playing with a construction site of colored Lego blocks. Simon, a fifth-grader and bright in technical matters, was helping him out. Mr. Toegel assessed the situation in just a few moments.

"Okay, Gernod," he said to his assistant, who had to stoop in order to not bump his head on the ceiling. "Set up right here in front of the piano. We want to hear this Chopin waltz again in a minute. Don't be shy, Mr. Pianist. What's your name again? Ah, that's right–Immanuel. All right then, start over please. It'll sound just fine. Gernod, come on. And, you guys, stay right where you were," he said to the kids who had come over. "It'll be your turn in a minute."

Everybody was mesmerized by the melody of his voice. Ernie himself was very skeptical toward the film producer and his intentions. He really didn't want to have anything to do with television and journalists. Yet, the more he watched him, the more impressed he became by the way Mr. Toegel went about his work. The girls at the big kitchen table were filmed. Then, the lights were focused on Lucky and his crane, which was almost finished. Thereafter, Mr. Toegel came over and put his hand on Simon's shoulder.

"Son, can you make a fire?"

Of course, Simon's eyes lit up brightly as if he were already looking into one.

"What about the fireplace? A warm, crackling fire would be a handy shot to have," said the director laughing. Even though it was snowing outside, the two men were perspiring. Their spotlights didn't just give off light but also heated up the low rooms in no time at all.

Simon knelt in front of the fireplace with wood, wood chips and paper. He opened the door, placing everything in nicely. He looked into the camera questioningly. Was the camera on already? Was anything missing? All eyes were on him. Mr. Toegel and Gernod exchanged a couple of words in their secret language. Toegel nodded for Simon to start. The first match broke; the second one did not catch fire. Although the third one made a hissing sound, it went out as soon as it was placed under the paper. What a flop! Unbelievable! Simon's heart pounded wildly. Don't give up now, he told himself. The camera was still making a whirring sound. The fourth match was a success. The flame was getting higher—and then died down the next moment. How could this happen to our pro?! Everyone was holding his breath. And everybody would see it all on film....

Even children can get nervous. Shaking a bit, Simon grabbed for the match box.

"It's got to work this time!" he thought to himself.

Carefully, his hand formed a shield around the little flame. He held it up next to the wood. The first twig began to glow. There was a spark, and Simon's eyes began to reflect the shine. The camera was still taking everything in. It turned out to be a splendid fire!

Now, Mr. Toegel had something else in mind. He surprised Hedi with a very direct question, "What do you think about all this?"

Hedi knew what he meant. He wasn't asking about her husband's work. He wanted to know what her feelings toward his frequent absences were. She felt a bit overwhelmed.

"I usually don't say anything, Mr. Toegel," she answered. "Let me think about it."

The following day, the film director found a note from Hedi. She had chosen to write out, rather than vocalize, her feelings:

> When we got married nineteen years ago, I knew that living with a preacher would mean a life of sacrifice. But, I had made a decision to say, "Yes." Still, knowing what that means in your head and actually living it out are two different things. A "yes" needs to be tested by fire in the everyday events of life. Every good-bye, every time of separation, every period of waiting were a result of my saying, "Yes."
>
> Often I was disappointed, impatient, angry, worried, in despair. Other times, I remained calm, happy, peaceful and full of faith. No one can predict how he is going to react in an emergency. Only in hindsight can I say that, even though some situations were rather hard and I did not make the grade in them, there was a wonderful force carrying me through. I have not regretted marrying Ernie Tanner.

Eleven years later, Hedi experienced another wave of farewells. The day her oldest daughter left her parents' house for an extended period of time, she wrote the following:

Farewell, farewell, farewell...On January 8, our "'little" girl flew into the jungles of Peru.... This morning our "big" Miriam flew to America with her husband....Tonight, Ernie is flying to Germany for twelve days....How does it feel, Hedi, when all of them leave and you have to stay at home? Sometimes, like a tree that has lost all its leaves–bare, naked. Sometimes I am a bit angry, sometimes sad, sometimes grateful, but every single time someone leaves, I feel lonesome. No one can help me in that. I almost want to quote Hesse, "Living means being alone." But I can't really say that. I *am* alone, that is true, but my life is fulfilling.

I am surrounded by the love of God. Therefore, saying farewell does not mean feeling miserable. It does hurt, but that is probably part of life. Life means coming and going, being in motion. Life is being alive. Children leave home because they are alive. They leave eager to experience something new. I'm so glad that my daughters are doing something for God. It is a farewell for them as well. They leave behind what is dear to them and plunge into a new adventure. Yes, farewells do cause pain, but it is the healthy kind. It can be healthy if we manage to stay positive.

The start of the air rally was scheduled for January 3. Twenty-three machines would be participating. The day arrived, seeming to be the foggiest of the entire year. You could hardly see your hand in front of your eyes. And flying? Not an option! Ernie was informed that some twin-engine aircrafts with sensitive instruments for such conditions were already on their way through the clouds across the Alps. Others were waiting impatiently for an opening in this thick white layer.

Ernie said good-bye to his loved ones. The orange jet helicopter behind the house of the Tanner family lifted off, quickly disappearing behind the clouds. Ten minutes later, the machine touched down again at the very same spot. It was impossible to get through.

"We'll try again tomorrow," Ernie decided.

Everyone was happy that Daddy would be home one more day. In fact, it turned out to be two. Not until January 5 would Ernie have a chance to get out of Trogen. Gernod, the camera man who was to film the rally, would accompany him. The Alps were still covered in thick clouds. The men tried to get to the Mediterranean Sea via Geneva and the Rhone River Valley. At about 3 p.m., they finally landed at the airport in Nice. They refueled quickly, and feeling slightly unsure, took a look at the Sea before daring to head for Corsica. During their flight, they were surprised by a radio message from one of the rally aircrafts. They agreed to wait for each other in Olbia, which was the next airport.

Visibility was very low as Ernie flew in the direction of Corsica. He followed the western coastline and then turned east across a vast plain before reaching the mountain range that separated the island from Sardinia. It was a miracle that the chopper could slip through an opening in the thick layer of clouds. Ernie had no time to celebrate his success: a storm was heading through the narrow sea passage as if passing through a funnel. It hit his helicopter hard and incessantly. As best he could, he clutched onto the controls, trying to keep that baby steady. Below him, wild, white breakers pounded against the jagged, black rocks of the coast.

Rather concerned, Ernie kept looking all around and checking his watch. According to his time schedule, he was supposed to be in Olbia soon. He switched on his radio, "Olbia Tower, this is Helicopter Hotel Bravo X-ray Delta Yankee. Do you read?" He listened closely. No reply. Then he tried to set his Navigation Direction Beacon (NDB) on Olbia. The light would not come on. His speed continued to plummet. With every bit of strength he had, he kept fighting against the stormy eastern wind. Finally, he was able to turn the machine in a southwesterly direction and follow the eastern coast of Sardinia. The wind had subsided a bit. Still, Ernie was concerned because twilight was setting in.

"If Olbia doesn't pop up within the next few minutes, I'll have to land," Ernie informed Gernod over headset. "The visibility is catastrophic."

Up until then, he had remained perfectly calm, despite all of the detours and difficult flight maneuvers due to the hazardous conditions. He had trusted Ernie to govern the helicopter. Now he began looking down nervously. Where in the world did he want to land? On the right hand side, the rocky coastline descended steeply into the Mediterranean Sea; on the left hand side, there was a wide expanse without a horizon.

The chopper sank lower and made a curve. Gernod looked past Ernie and saw the mountains coming toward them. They looked uninhabited and cold. Then, they raced past a single white building. Ernie made a circle, heading toward the water, but flying more slowly. There were a few houses there, built very close to each other. There was something shiny between them. Was this a spot where they could land? No, it wasn't! There was a boat on it! Its lights were being reflected on the water.

Ernie switched on his own lights, got the 'copter's nose up again and flew toward the mountain one more time. He fixed them upon a white house down there. He could see a large square in front of it. It seemed to be the only possible place for a landing. He hovered over the village, evaluating everything carefully. He saw people walking around and switching the lights off and on.

"Hold on, Gernod, we're going to land on the hotel terrace," Ernie said.

Approaching from the seaside, he inched closer, descending carefully. He hovered briefly and touched down. They were back on terra firma. He took a deep breath and shut off the turbine to cool off. It was 5:50

p.m. on a very dark winter evening. They had flown for over two hours until daylight had given way to nightfall.

"Man, look at the Christmas tree!" Gernod said, amused, looking out of the window.

Ernie had not seen it upon landing. Now it was too late. The wind from the rotor blades had blown it over. There it was, beaten up and lying on the washed-out stone floor.

Where were they? Surprised faces were staring their way, wanting to find out who the big shots were who had come without making reservations. Ernie got out of the helicopter, walked up to the first person, and in his rusty Italian, apologized profusely for the incident with the Christmas tree. Questions went back and forth until a tall man appeared. He said he was a police officer, although not in uniform, and wanted to see their passports.

Now, the "direttore" (manager) of the "albergo" (hotel) wanted to know how heavy the machine was. How long was it going to stay on his terrace? He took Ernie and Gernod down a level to a small grocery store. The terrace rested on its pillars. After inspecting things thoroughly, Ernie assured the man that there were no cracks or other damage. Ernie did notice that, to his surprise, he had landed directly on top of the main beam, meaning the little "negozio" (store) had been spared major damage.

Finally they landed in Olbia. Bruno, the pilot of the small aircraft who had radioed Ernie the day before, couldn't resist teasing him.

"Hello, you Swiss Chopper One air force dudes, where have you been all this time?"

"Captain Tanner attempted a foolhardy, dangerous emergency landing to spend the night in a luxury hotel in Porto Cervo," Gernod answered, laughing.

"Well, we can't keep going at that pace," Bruno replied. "Today we'll take you with us and cross the ocean in formation."

"In case of an emergency landing, the rescue helicopter will be right there, too," Ernie said cheerfully.

Usually, the long flight across the desert was a lonely one. The idea of having company this time around was like a shot in the arm to Ernie. How often had he missed having someone around in the air to stay in radio contact with? It would be much easier to make decisions as a team and to have someone there for any hard calls. Would it really work out?

The agreement was for all of the aircrafts to meet in Djarba, Tunisia. They would spend the evening there together. The two machines took off from Olbia, lifting off into the heat of day shortly after noon. It was reassuring for Ernie to see the small machine with the Swiss cross in front of him. It did him good to be able to exchange a few words now and then with Bruno. They had drawn up the flight schedule together since Bruno had excellent instruments on board.

Ernie leaned back in his seat, relishing the moment. He stuck to his course, keeping his eyes on the man in front of him. Now he had time to talk with Gernod, who had his camera and audio recorder ready to go at all times. He was jerked back into reality when, unexpectedly, two planes were flying in front of him instead of just one. Another rally machine? No! A Tunisian military fighter plane took the lead in front of Bruno, turned abruptly and indicated clearly to follow him. Shocked, Ernie consulted his map. They had penetrated a military zone. What should they do now? He turned and tried to leave the zone. At that same moment, he was greeted by an army helicopter. He was required to follow them and landed right behind Bruno on a military base. What a rude awakening after such sweet dreams of a peaceful flight!

Things were finally hopping at the control tower of Djarba Airport. For two days now, German and Swiss machines of all sizes and types had been landing there. With a satisfied look, the flight controller regarded the long line of silver birds all parked nicely next to each other, gleaming in the sunlight. Another one had already contacted them by radio. The airstrip was clear.

"Let him land then. Blast it! This is number twenty-two. Two are still missing!"

The man in the tower was counting.

"Seems like they've got nothing else to do but jet around!"

He looked over to the group of people standing around, talking, discussing and gesticulating as they waited. He seemed to be envious.

One man was wearing a smart, bright safari outfit. He went from one group to the other. It was Mr. Henseler, the rally organizer. Over and over again, he would look up into the clear blue sky and point to the long row of planes. Then, with a firm look in his eyes, he would march up to the plane that had just landed.

"Hey, there. Did you have a good flight? Which direction did you come from? What was the weather like? Did you meet anybody? No radio contact?"

He was obviously on edge. The two men introduced themselves, smiling, and added, "Well, over Corsica we did hear something on the radio. I think it was a helicopter. The pilot said something like, 'Olbia, wait.' We didn't hear with whom he was in contact. Has he not arrived yet?"

Rubbing his hands nervously, Mr. Henseler looked at his watch.

"When was that, you said? Yesterday? The day before? Just a moment please. Let me check with the tower."

Once again, Mr. Henseler did a head count: twenty-two. The helicopter and pilot were missing, even though he supposedly knew the way. Henseler had to check with Olbia. Determined, he made his way over to the tower.

The afternoon passed. The sun was going down on the horizon. Finally, Tunis acknowledged that a helicopter had both landed and then taken off that day. Almost simultaneously, they heard aircraft noise. The missing duo appeared in the evening sky. What a welcome Ernie, Gernod and Bruno got upon their arrival! A big hurray!

In the end, everything had worked out just fine. All were ready to do some serious celebrating.

Two days later, it was time to leave the desert behind. A few of the rally pilots met up in Kano, Nigeria. There they got some bad news: one machine had been forced to land in the desert with engine trouble. It desperately needed new parts. Ernie was more than glad to contact Switzerland via HF radio to order them. Then mid-afternoon, he hit the ignition and took off to Maroua, Cameroon. He tuned in the frequency, saying, "Radio Berna, Radio Berna, this is helicopter Hotel Bravo X-ray Delta Yankee, do you read?" No reply. He flew higher and higher, attempting to contact Switzerland the whole time. He kept an eye on his compass to stay on course. Finally, at 12,000 ft., he connected with Switzerland, giving them his home phone number. Only seconds later, he heard Hedi's voice.

"Can you hear me?"

"Faintly."

"I am on my way from Kano to Maroua at 12,000 feet. I need spare parts for a German machine. You got that?"

"Yeah, kind of."

Ernie then had to repeat the address as well as the number of the spare parts several times before Hedi fully got it. It was laborious. The turbine noise and the wind conditions rendered a normal conversation virtually impossible. Radio Berna had to cut off the connection since their words were being totally distorted. At least Ernie had been able to convey the message. What a comfort! But where was he now? How much time had passed? The bleak landscape below him seemed endless, and now it was covered with an impenetrable fog. He descended further and further. There was not much left for his companion-in-flight Gernod to do. Filming was impossible, but he had done enough of that the days before. He exchanged a few words with Ernie off and on, giving him some snacks. He looked at the flight map and calculated how long they still had to go.

"I've got to try to reach Radio Berna again. We won't make it to Maroua before nightfall. We lost too much time going up."

Ernie switched on the radio.

"Radio Berna!"

They actually heard him.

"Please reconnect me with Trogen...Hello, Hedi, can you hear me?"

"A bit. What's up?"

"We have to land in the desert. Dusk is overtaking us already. In case the folks from the rally are looking for us, please tell them we'll be there tomorrow. Did you get that?"

"You're going to be in Maroua tomorrow. All right. Happy landing. Over."

The helicopter was flying lower and lower, heading toward the inhospitable wasteland. Still no landmark. You could no longer see the sun. The earth coming toward them seemed sinister and hostile. Was that a light down there? It became more and more visible. A fire! How wonderful! Ernie landed, greeting the people. He indicated they wanted to spend the night there. It meant going to sleep hungry....

The next day Ernie and Gernod were up at the break of dawn and ready for takeoff. Ernie didn't know much, only that they had gotten totally off course due to strong upper winds. He flew at a high altitude to get his bearings. He discovered a large body of water in the distance. It had to be Lake Chad. He turned south and reached Maroua after three hours and ten minutes. They were being eagerly awaited there.

The flight from Trogen to Yaounde, including all of their detours, had taken thirty-eight hours. In Cameroon itself, Ernie flew with the camera team first. Later on, during a fifty-two-day period, he piloted one hundred and fifty missions in conjunction with Georg Ackermann. He had thereby increased his flight experience to a total of 1,450 hours. He had crisscrossed Cameroon from the north to the south and from the east to the west. Ernie had been able to serve people in the remotest of places in all kinds of invaluable ways.

A copy of Mr. Toegel's film entitled *Help from the Air* was sent to him as promised. Ernie was able to present it to his friends in Switzerland that same fall.

Chapter 30
Sunny Start–Dreary End

The year 1978 brought Ernie new opportunities to utilize and new difficulties to overcome. On January 9, he signed the purchasing order for a BO 105 in Munich. It was powerful and fast, a beautiful blue and red twin-engine machine, especially useful in the exceptionally high mountains of Bolivia.

In March, he participated in a one-week training course offered by its manufacturer. This gave him the "book theory" about the bird. In April, he took seventeen lessons in Samaden, Switzerland, to brush up his flying. Those lessons in the Engadine valley were hard ones. The glacial area of Bernina was more his cup of tea. Landing on peaks, however, made him slightly dizzy. Wolf, his friend and instructor, didn't give him any breaks. Every chance to get practice at those altitudes was mercilessly seen through.

On April 16, a cold, unpleasant spring day, the new machine, named HB-XHE, was dedicated in Sitterdorf. The weather did not deter Ernie from chauffeuring around many friends of Helimission on a short sightseeing tour. Wolf also demonstrated his flying expertise, which left many onlookers with their mouths open. They also appreciated an exhibition with more details about Africa.

On May 8, Ernie left for Hamburg. From there, "the BO" was taken to Philadelphia onboard a container ship. Its transfer from America to Bolivia started on June 3. Nick was chosen to be its new pilot. It took twelve days for them to fly southward over Texas, Mexico, Central America, Panama, Columbia and Peru, finally landing in La Paz, Bolivia. In those twelve days, Ernie's collection of stampmarks in his logbook from many small and large airports grew quickly!

A few days later, Nick's wife arrived in Bolivia on a commercial flight from America. Together, the couple made Cochabamba, a city of 150,000 known for its pleasant climate, their home. However, the initial joy was short-lived. On October 16, they left Bolivia, the helicopter and their missionary work behind without notice. Ernie heard through the grapevine that Nick's wife had been unable to adjust to the lifestyle in Bolivia.

Thus, the beautiful BO 105 had to wait six months for a new pilot. Joe, a cowboy from Arizona, arrived on May 16, 1979. He was a friendly man of few words. He landed in Cochabamba with his wife, three sons, two daughters and a six-foot mountain of luggage. He was ready to serve on the mission field. He also brought a great amount of experience with him, consisting of nearly 8,000 flight hours on six different types of helicopters. For sixteen months, he flew missionaries into the villages situated high up in the Andes Mountains. One of the missionaries was Homer Firestone, an old pioneer missionary. He would wear a hat with a wide brim on his head, tuck a Bible under his arm and go preach in Chulpani, a nearly deserted mountain village.

Joe took other missionaries to the jungle and swamp areas of the Beni River. Among the natives there were the pioneers of the New Tribes Mission. Keth Benson, an evangelist from Venezuela, had received a warm welcome by the chief of an American Indian settlement. He said he had been desiring for a priest to come and preach in his village. He drummed all of his tribesmen together, that is, forty-two persons. All of them listened intently to the message of God's love.

In October 1980, Joe, his wife and his two daughters moved to Santiago de Chile. They wanted to aid missionaries there in reaching southern Chile with the Gospel. Their sons, then ages sixteen, eighteen and twenty, moved back to Arizona. Ernie visited the family in Santiago. They explored the southern part of Chile with the helicopter. They visited missions headquarters and preached the Good News to the natives. They also presented the unlimited possibilities of using the helicopter to missionaries there. Some were fascinated; some, skeptical. Ernie and Joe were impressed and moved by the beauty of the craggy Pacific coastline. They had the joy of viewing volcanoes, waterfalls and huge, veldt-like plains in the inland. Ernie ached to bring the love of God to those people, to visit all those small villages. For the time being, however, it had to suffice to "spy out the land." He had to leave the evangelistic tasks to the missionary societies based there.

Unfortunately, this was the reason why "Mission Chile" may have failed. Either Joe wasn't the man to explain the advantages of the helicopter to the missionaries, or they didn't want to part from their traditional ways. Maybe they didn't have the budget for using choppers - at the price of fuel! Maybe the home committees failed to see the purpose in it. Good ole "BO" was on the ground more than in the air. There were also different administrative and technical problems. Joe's enthusiasm gradually dwindled away. His reports were simply a list of things to worry about, and they became few and far between. When their three-year contract expired, Joe and his wife did not feel they could continue working for Helimission.

Then real difficulties began setting in. Ernie had the prospect of employing another pilot, but, in the end, it didn't work out after all. Although "the BO" was safely parked at the Carabineros, that is, the police station in Santiago, it lay heavy on Ernie's conscience that it was standing still. What should they do? Keep waiting? Just let "BO" sit there? Rent it out? Sell it? A solution had to come.

Chapter 31
Success in Cameroon–Fighting in Kenya

In Cameroon, where Helimission had first been established, there were problems as well. Several pilots had come and gone. The burning question of the moment was what the best location for the base should be. This meant it was time for another large building project. To Ernie's great surprise, several young men from his homeland approached him. They were good with their hands and ready to use their skills on the mission field. Georg, who had already accompanied Ernie previously, was the first to volunteer.

Helimission was able to purchase some land in Bamenda. It was situated next to the Full Gospel Mission with a gorgeous view over the valley. Peter Schneider, an architect and missionary, became Ernie's neighbor–and architect. Georg, Hansruedi, Roebi, and Michael were the names of the four enthusiastic construction workers. The house went up quickly, and the new pilot's family was delighted with their lovely new home. One year later, the helicopter also got its hangar next door. The facilities have, since then, been host to great joy and happiness with many people coming and going, moving in and moving out. They became a meeting place for missionaries from a large spectrum of missionary societies. The house and the helicopter were always available for them all. One of the HM (Helimission) pilots wrote about his time there:

I fly doctors and nurses for the Baptists to the bush clinics. I also make flights for the Evangelical-Lutheran Church, taking mostly evangelists to the Koma tribes. (This was a tribe which Ernie first encountered in 1977; he was the first white man to stay in contact with them.) The missionaries stay there for two months. When the time is up, I bring a couple of new missionaries there and take the other ones back. Once, I stayed with the Koma for a week myself. Pastor Farestad, a doctor, the African pastor Norbert, as well as two other pastors were present as well. We preached in their services, baptized ten believers, treated the sick and counseled them on different issues. We were able to relay messages from government officials, for example, that they were concerned about the Moslems persecuting the Koma people. They intended to work toward a solution to the problem. The Lamido, a Moslem chief, that is, had been reprimanded and had received a fine. Meanwhile, it was required of all of the Koma to register officially and come pick up identity cards. This meant leaving their entrusted mountain terrain and coming down into the valley. However, the Koma tribesmen didn't really trust the government to keep its promise. Many of the families have, in the meantime, received Jesus as their Redeemer. Their standard of living has improved. Two of the families are even attending Bible School in Tibati. Soon, they'll be preaching the Gospel to their own people.

Ernie had petitioned the government for a radio transmission permit. He hoped to facilitate better communication between hospitals and the missions headquarters. Years later, he had practically given up hope in getting a positive reply. Just then, he received the approval for seven radio transmission stations. He purchased the necessary equipment in Switzerland. He took a short course-half a day it lasted-in assembling antennae. Then he ordered the radio devices from America. After waiting so long, he managed to pull everything together at the drop of a hat. Then he traveled to Cameroon, lugging the heavy equipment there. He flew from one mission station to the other, climbed up the roofs and set up the antennae, mostly on his own.

When the first signal to the hospital in Ngoundere was confirmed, everyone celebrated! Every morning, the various mission stations received their call from Bamenda at an appointed time. But who would man this new tool once Ernie returned home? For the time being, things were quiet since their pilot had just returned to the States.

Ernie was looking for someone who spoke English and French and had the necessary time, vim and vigor to find their way around in far-off Africa. Ernie decided to ask Trudy, a retired secretary in a neighboring village. During World War II, Trudy had worked as a driver for the Red Cross. She was a courageous, energetic woman, who wore her age very well although she was already over seventy.

"Okay, Ernie, I'll go, but only if you can't find anybody else!" was her spontaneous answer. She added a bit more pensively, "However, someone will have to take care of my house and my pets. There are the cats, the rabbits and my collie Zita. Actually, I can't really live without her. She is almost as old as I am. It would be hard for her to get used to someone else."

Amused, Ernie patted her on her shoulder encouragingly and replied, "If you go, Zita will join you."

Time passed, and it was just before midnight when the phone rattled Hedi awake. She picked up the receiver sleepily, murmuring an unhappy "Tanners' residence" into the receiver.

"Hello, Hedi, please forgive me for calling so late."

It was Ernie on the other end of the line. Something had gone wrong–that much was clear–for he would not disturb her well-deserved sleep otherwise.

"Did Trudy make it over all right?" his wife asked anxiously. They had arranged for him to pick her up at the airport in Douala.

"Oh, yes, Trudy did, but Zita didn't. Hedi, would you please call Geneva? Trudy had to change planes there. Maybe they put Zita on the next plane there. I'll call back in fifteen minutes."

So Hedi called Cointrin Airport in the middle of the night. However, it took another two days before Trudy, at her wits' end, was able to stroke her beloved Zita again. Ernie then trained Trudy for her new job. She learned quickly and cheerfully. After only two weeks, she was the singular mistress of the house in Bamenda, well-protected by Zita. After someone else took over, she returned to Switzerland and told her story:

One day, Ernie Tanner told me he was urgently looking for someone to take over the management of the new radio facilities in Cameroon. I was speechless when he said he had been thinking about me since I spoke English and French. I had my doubts, but Mr. Tanner encouraged me several times to take this step anyhow. Thus, on August 31 of last year, I left for the Black Continent. It was totally foreign to me. My fears were legitimate: I was to live on an isolated hill, though beautifully situated, on my own—no neighbors and no telephone. Letters would take two to three weeks to reach home. My health was not at its best all the time, and I would have to cope with the new climate. I have to admit that my trust in God was wobbly. But it became stronger and stronger as I received His help during emergencies. Sometimes things looked hopeless, but the Lord was always there when I called on Him. I would like to take this opportunity to say thank-you to all those who prayed for me. The mission was worth it. Working with radio and having daily contact with the various missionaries, some in far-off places, was a pleasure. Over the course of time, I met a lot of precious people who have become good friends since. I can only encourage young people to not focus on their problems but make themselves available to the Lord for the mission field.

The news from Kenya sounded quite different. The pilot named Van got permission to fly his helicopter to Uganda as well. He flew the representative of "Christian Aid" to the missions headquarters in Kaabong. He was to verify whether aid needed to be flown in to the Karamoja area. It took only one flight to convince him of it! Van also suggested that "Christian Aid" take part in financially supporting the use of the helicopter. It would be indispensable in that region. Unfortunately, his recommendation was not accepted by the decision-makers.

In Trogen, everyone read Van's reports with the greatest of interest. In Karamoja in the northeastern part of Uganda, the situation was terrible. One of his reports offered details:

> The Ugandan church asked me to fly to the bush hospital. From there, I was to pick up a badly injured man. He had been driving a truckload of food supplies when he had been overcome by thieves. They shot him in the back and in the head. He could not be transported normally due to bad road conditions, so I flew him to Entebbe. From there, an ambulance drove him to the hospital. Every month, about a hundred new patients come to this bush hospital. Three-quarters have been victimized by robbers. I also visited a camp that offers food to the hungry. Due to terrorist activities, the farmers were unable to plant crops. Plus, their livestock was continually being stolen. It's no wonder that they are starving to death. Today, I'll be flying to Kaabong to bring sorely needed intravenous needles to the medical team of "Save the Children." Tomorrow, I'll fly an UNICEF secretary over there to assess the situation. Hopefully he'll approve the resumption of those food transports!

Van was only able to carry out the first assignment. During the second one, he was attacked and forced to return to Kenya. This was his report:

> I intended to land at Sotori Airport to pick up the UNICEF secretary. Hovering barely six feet above the ground, I thought I heard bullets flying. I remember thinking, "They can't be shooting at me!" Then, I heard another bang. I put the pedal to the metal and got out of there as fast as I could. I managed to escape through a space between the hangar and the trees, which offered some protection. For about five seconds, I gave it all I had. I remember the unusual noise the turbine made. I flew twenty miles into the bush. Then, I landed and spent the night there. The following morning, I checked the chopper for bullet holes but didn't find any, thank God! Then, I carried out an inspection and also examined the bird for any other signs of overtaxing. I couldn't check the turbine since I am not qualified to do that. I didn't have any tools for that either. Had I left the machine to go look for a qualified mechanic, the Tanzanian "liberators" could have destroyed or confiscated it. Since the helicopter appeared to be operable, I decided to return to Kenya. I landed in Kitale, the nearest possible city, with only five gallons left in the fuel tank.

Reports like this were not very encouraging for Ernie. He had watched the news and learned that a Swiss helicopter had been shot at in Uganda. After the damaged jet engine had been fixed, Van proceeded with his relief flights in Uganda.

The report of a nurse specialized in treating eye diseases showed another side of the helicopter mission in Kenya. She phrased it a bit like a radio message from up in the air:

MISSION UNREACHABLE is underway beginning October 25. Come in, please. This is HB-XCH, an aircraft from the Helimission fleet on assignment for Mission for the Blind. A team of eye specialists is on board. We are approaching Kapsowar at 7,875 ft. above sea level. We are two-and-a-half flight hours out of Nairobi. Visibility is clear. The Kapsowar missions headquarters are located on a plateau, and we are approaching. There seems to be a football field down there. About one hundred school kids are assembling quickly. Blue school uniforms are all over. There is so much activity–it looks as if the mountain slopes are coming alive. The kids are waving at us with pink slips. What could that be? Ready for landing. Over.

October 27. Come in, please. This is HB-XCX of Helimission on assignment for Mission for the Blind. MISSION UNREACHABLE was a success! Do you read? We are leaving Kapsowar right now. Visibility is low, numerous clouds. The eye team is fine. I repeat: this is HB-XCX on behalf of Mission for the Blind. MISSION UNREACHABLE accomplished! We are approaching Eldoret. Lots of cloud coverage, but everything else is okay. Get the bathtub ready. The pilot has dirty feet! End of message. Over and out!"

Next to flying, the most important ministry of a pilot is working together with other missionaries. The helicopter can only be employed to the maximum if he is able to coordinate missions. One also has to foster fellowship with others and keep the contacts he has. Organizing the flights is one thing; encouraging missionaries to make use of the available machine for missions is another. Some assignments would be impossible without it. Often, missionaries are so busy training, building, preaching and writing that they forget there are other people "beyond the mountains" as well. Helimission was called into being for them: for people waiting for help...and for those missionary pioneers willing to bring it.

Chapter 32

The Family Comes Along

For Hedi and the children, it was a great joy to accompany Ernie on one of his trips. Nothing could help them grasp the full scope of his endeavors more. Yes, they'd heard their father's stories time and time again. Yet there was no replacement for seeing him in action firsthand.

The earthquake took place on a Sunday night. Gino, a volunteer from Salerno, said later on that it had lasted only ninety seconds. At the epicenter, the duration was 120 seconds. The earth's rumbling, the sudden darkness, the sudden blast and people screaming–it must have been horrible.

Ernie didn't hear about the disaster in the news until days after it had happened. He immediately sensed a heavy burden on his heart for the people there. After all, he was equipped to help, wasn't he? The machine from Cameroon was waiting right behind his house. It had come home for a thorough checkup in Switzerland. Ernie got on the phone, offering his services to many organizations. Some said no; others, yes. Some inquired further; others couldn't make up their minds. There were many "buts" and "what ifs." In the meantime, Ernie did not lose time in getting the chopper ready. After a suspenseful week, he finally received an official invitation to come. At the same time, the German Red Cross in Naples granted him flight permission.

The cooperation with the Red Cross was very positive. Ernie was able to reach numerous places despite inclement weather. He was able to relay important information to the coordination office, which meant help could come more efficiently. For the last two days of his mission, he and a Swiss missionary from Salerno visited many of the villages hardest hit. They established important contacts. In his many conversations, he perceived a great spiritual need in the people's lives.

On December 12, Ernie returned home. He suggested to his family that they spend Christmas in southern Italy. Everybody agreed willingly. Only Hedi was apprehensive. Even before his leaving for the disaster relief operation, she had asked Ernie if he minded seeing dead people.

"Do you know what to say to people who are desperate or near death?" she wanted to know.

He didn't mind seeing the dead. Yes, he knew what to tell people and what to do. Seeing misery and death was not new. He had encountered them in Ethiopia. He was confident and wanted nothing more than to bring help. Ten days remained until Christmas. Ernie wanted to write an appeal flyer and have it translated and printed. He wanted to ask companies to donate products for about 2,000 packages.

In the days that followed, nothing seemed to work out. Ernie and Hedi were about to give up. Then, one morning, Hedi's youngest son left a note on his freshly-made bed which was still warm. It read, "For the helicopter mission to Italy." Enclosed were three bills of twenty Swiss-Francs each. Those were his entire savings! If he could believe in the mission, then Ernie and Hedi wanted to believe in it, too.

From that moment on, each day brought a new, positive surprise. By Saturday, they could hardly find the desks in the office. There were mountains of boxes everywhere. Tables were lined up in a long row. Volunteers were busily filling 2,000 bags in assembly-line fashion. Donations included pens, candles, sewing kits, toothpaste, deodorant, matches, torches, cookies, nuts, candy and chocolate. Of course, a small letter with words of comfort went into each bag as well. The packages totaling about 2,200 pounds were transported by bus. Ernie hooked a camper onto his car, loaded with musical instruments, luggage, and, of course, the children. They left Trogen early on December 23. Around 1 a.m. after a long, grueling ride, the family sank exhausted into their beds at the hotel. Ernie had stayed there during his first mission.

Hedi and the children shared their impressions of the tiring but eventful days that followed:

The sun shone brightly over Salerno. It glistened over the ocean as I stepped out on the balcony Christmas morning. We loaded up the vehicle with great joy in our hearts. Ernie sat in front, along with Gino, our Italian friend and interpreter. Miriam, Damaris, Simon and I sat in the middle. Lukas sat in the back, squeezed in between the camera, picnic items, coats and instruments. Ernie was expecting the best as he checked out the route to the devastated areas. We had even tied boxes with small Christmas gifts onto the roof of the car.

After about one-and-a-half hours, we reached a mountain range. The view from there was marvelous. The road itself was quite torn up. Close by, we saw a trailer parked in front of a deserted house that had collapsed. A farmer was tending to his sheep and cows. A couple of children followed up the herd behind him. We gave each of them a box. We watched as for a moment their little faces, overshadowed by shock and fear, lit up.

We drove on to St. Andrea. We were supposed to meet a gentleman at a gas station who would show us where to park the camper. After waiting for a long time, we began asking around. Finally, we found the man. He got into our car as well, making it rather tight for all of us. He led us by way of serpentine roads through the valley to Caposele. He had a brother there. He and his wife had been living in a tiny Fiat since the earthquake. The camper was for them. We parked it next to others in a large lot and then we showed them to their new "home." They were very, very grateful.

Then, in St. Angelo, we visited a family living in a metal container. They cooked over a fire they had made directly on the ground. The place was filled with smoke. Our eyes smarted from it. A baby was crying. Ernie prayed for them. We felt at a loss for words, but we did shed a few tears.

The scene in the village is breaking our hearts, too. Everybody wants us to come over to their "home" to show us their miserable conditions. One person talks with our girls; another, with the boys. We say, "Coraggio" ("Don't lose heart") and "Vi amiamo" ("We love you"). At times, we can say nothing at all. We simply embrace and kiss them. We also shake many hands. Often, we just stand close to them, taking things in, listening to their cares.

In Lioni, we visit the "people on the train." A chicken ladder with wide rungs leads up to the door in the middle of a wagon. The other wagons have no access doors. There are no lights, and twilight is setting in. One wagon appears to be deserted, parked on an unused track with a few others. Is anyone in the world living in there? We see no one and start to go in. A soldier tries to hold us back. Ernie attempts to explain the situation, holding out the letter of reference from the Red Cross. A friendly nurse turns up and allows us to come inside. This wagon of the train has been coverted into a sick bay. We distribute our boxes, singing Christmas songs and Italian choruses. People's faces beam. The nurse asks us to sing some songs in the next wagon also. The volunteers form a circle, sitting next to the patients, just listening. It is Christmas day. All of us are richly blessed.

Hedi

As a result of our visit, many desperate people received fresh hope and courage. By distributing tracts, we had a chance to bring the Gospel to many devastated families. We were able to show them that God loves them despite their ill-fortune. I believe we should regard their fate as our own and truly intercede for these dear people.

Miriam

Placing himself in the position of one of the earthquake victims, one of the Tanner boys shares what is going through the person's mind:

The earth trembles beneath my feet. People are yelling. Dust is flying around everywhere. Houses collapse with a loud crash. My own house is just a heap now. My guinea pig has run away. My cattle and my sheep, my dog and my pussy cat are buried somewhere under the remains of the stable. They bark and meow. It breaks my heart, but I cannot save them. Where is my bird? It has escaped!

My father lies underneath the rubble of the house. My mother has been fatally injured. My brother has been smashed to bits in the car. My sister is dead. This is my family situation now. All I have is a camper, just a small camper. Food is being brought to me, but that's all. No one is asking me about my father or mother. About my siblings. No one is there to comfort me. There is no loving person at my side...to just be with me... to encourage me through this time and give me hope. There is no one to explain how this terrible tragedy fits into the plan laid out in the Bible. I'm all alone. It feels like a knife stabbing me; yet, God is on my side. I'm alive, but my father and mother and brothers and sisters are dead. How my heart yearns for some word of comfort...of love! Is this supposed to be Christmas?

Simon

The youngest Tanner boy tells it as only a child can:

We drove through the city of Lioni. There, I saw lots of things which stuck with me. In one apartment block, the whole side had sagged down about three feet. The connecting beams were all torn up. I saw a house where you could only see the upper floor; the rest had sunk into the ground. In another house I saw the living room lampshade hanging from the ceiling because the outer wall had collapsed. I could look into a lot of rooms where only the furniture was left in one piece, but you couldn't go inside. It would have been too dangerous–the house could have collapsed over your head. The worst thing was that the people looked so sad because they didn't know why all of this had happened.

Lukas

Laviano was one of the last villages we visited. Like most others, it was situated on top of a hill. Standing at the foot of the hill at twilight, we looked at the village as one big heap of rubble. The road went straight up the hill and was in terrible shape. From what we understood, this village had been waiting for help longer than any other since the access road had been partially buried under debris. The expression on the faces of the people standing around left a deep mark on my heart. The closer we came to the village, the more shaken up I was by the sight. I hadn't seen this much anguish leading up to this point in time.

We parked our car on the edge of the village and then walked over to it. I could hardly tell where houses had stood before: debris was everywhere. Soldiers had been able to clear very small paths. Patiently, they had picked up one stone after the other, searching for missing inhabitants. This certainly must have been one of the most terrible jobs. No perfume could have been strong enough to cover up the stench of dead bodies. Off and on again, we met people still looking for their belongings. Others could no longer cope with the sight of their once beautiful mountain village now destroyed. In various places, there were coffins heaped up, waiting to give the missing persons their final rest. There was a cat sitting on one of the debris heaps in the center of the village; it couldn't bear to leave the area it knew so well.

Later, we drove down to the villagers at the foot of the hill. All of them had found temporary shelter in a trailer. We met a young man who cried out in despair, "Everything is gone! The house. The family. Everything!" He grabbed our daddy and hugged him. Then he left him standing there and ran into the trailer. We waited for him to come back. He did return, holding out a book toward us. Its title was *Azzurro*. It was a collection of poems he had written about his village, its people, his homeland, his school. He was a teacher. What providence! We were given the book to take home with us. We had many possibilities to share a good word with the people so shaken up there. Their hearts were yearning for something. We were able to bring a song of peace and watched as part of their dire thirst for help was quenched. Almost everywhere we went, the people greeted us warmly.

Damaris

The entire Tanner family was up and about from dawn until dusk. They learned how to persevere under tough circumstances. They also experienced a satisfaction and joy which rewarded their efforts. One week later, they all got out of the car at home. Although worn out, all agreed that it had been the best Christmas they had ever had.

The following summer, the Tanner family returned to the disaster area. Ernie visited the places where he had seen so much agony. He met many familiar faces again. This time he did not come bearing gifts, but he still found friends who gladly welcomed him and his loved ones back.

Part Five

Chapter 33
Barbalo

It was warm outside although the date was January 14, 1983. The spring mood didn't quite match that of Ernie Tanner, who was just getting off the subway on 43rd Street in New York City. He took in a deep breath of the mild air and let out a heavy sigh. The look in his eyes, though, revealed determination to accomplish what he had come for. Hurriedly, he pressed through the crowd. His thoughts carried him far away from this city, which he knew so well, down to Chile. The beautiful BO 105 had been causing him headaches there for quite some time now. It was the reason he was here in New York.

Joe, the pilot of the BO 105 in South America, had endured a three-year trial of his patience. Eventually, he had gotten tired of the lack of interest in helicopter use by the missions organizations. He returned to his home country on short notice. Ernie knew only too well what he had gone through and could not blame Joe. Now he was wondering what should happen next. Should he find a new home for the chopper? Should he leave it there and let people charter it until a new pilot was found? Would a new door open soon? He had been to Chile himself, and had flown the BO 105 from Temuco to Santiago. It was now parked at the Carabineros, the police station.

Word that people could charter or even buy the helicopter got around quickly. Soon enough, the first few offers came in. A certain Mr. Griffin from Santiago showed an interest. On the same day, a New York company which had signed a contract for an oil platform in southern Chile called Ernie. They wanted to lease or buy a twin-engine machine. Since Ernie had been invited to preach in the United States, he took the opportunity to visit this company.

Now he remembered the telephone conversation. In the course of it, he had mentioned that a Mr. Griffin from

Santiago had also made him an offer. The gentleman
on the phone immediately discouraged him, saying he
knew that man Griffin. Under no circumstances should
Ernie agree to payments via New York, London or Paris.
Instead he should insist on payments via a bank in Chile;
otherwise, he might get dragged into a money laundering
affair. Ernie had communicated these conditions to
Santiago. He did not hear another word from Griffin.

At the thought of this, he drew in a sharp breath. He
was certain that God had protected him from harrowing
consequences. He walked even faster. The appointment
at that company was to take place today. The man from
the phone conversation wasn't there. His boss, however,
a man called Fernando Rios Selvo de Barbalo, wanted to
meet him. Ernie made his way to Fifth Avenue, the seat
of some of the most prominent companies in the world.

He went up to the twenty-fourth floor. A friendly
older lady welcomed him in and led him into the spacious
office of the boss. Ernie was quite surprised when a
charming man in his thirties, a somewhat shorter fellow,
greeted him. He had expected the boss of this large
company to be older. The man's low and quiet voice and
his confident behavior, however, left no doubt about his
competence. After a tour of the many offices, Ernie and
he sat down facing a window with a panoramic view of
the world-famous business center of Manhattan.

"I've got some interesting news," blurted out Mr.
Barbalo, getting down to business. "A Mr. Griffin offered
to sell us a BO 105. We inquired at the representative
office for BOs here. Mr. Moore, who knows you personally,
assured me it could only be your machine, Mr. Tanner.
It is the only BO 105 in all of Chile owned by a private
party."

Ernie understood in a second: this man Griffin
wanted to sell Ernie's prized chopper before they had
even come to an agreement–let alone before he had paid
for it!

"Without letting Mr. Griffin know what I know," Mr. Barbalo continued, "I've arranged for him to come here tomorrow to draw up the purchase agreement. Once he is here, I'll have you confront him. We'll uncover his trick. He's going to get here by 3 p.m."

Shocked and distressed about Griffin's hypocritical plan, Ernie was equally delighted in seeing the man exposed—and embarrassed. He talked with Mr. Barbalo about his helicopter missions in the Third World. The rich businessman was very impressed. He promised to support this interesting work as much as possible. He himself had studied law at a Jesuit university but had left just before finishing up. The two men moved to deeper spiritual matters. Business was soon forgotten. Finally Mr. Barbalo got up, giving him his business card. On it, Ernie read that Barbalo was working with *Evergreen*, one of the largest helicopter companies in the USA. He was their representative for Chile. Mr. Barbalo then insisted on treating Ernie to lunch. After eating at the Lincoln Hotel, he drove him to his apartment outside of New York in his Rolls Royce. Ernie shares the incident:

I'll never forget the trip. It has been indelibly etched into my mind. Mind you, I had never seen a Rolls Royce from the inside and now here we were, gliding along. The engine was smooth and quiet. We listened to Vivaldi on first-class speakers and were the envy of the other drivers. Barbalo didn't just enjoy the ride but also my obvious delight in conversing with him.

"These apartments belong to my company," Barbalo said, by the way as we stopped in front of three gigantic apartment blocks.

The vehicle drove down into the multilevel garage below the earth. We were welcomed by the porter, as is due the owner of the house. The lift took us up to the twenty-third floor. There, we entered Barbalo's private office where he introduced me to his assistant, Mr. Rain.

The view of New York at dusk was breathtaking.
I couldn't take my eyes off of it. I also met Barbalo's
wife and eight-year-old son. While he was going
through his mail, I drew a few pictures for the boy.

Later on, that unforgettable car took him back to the
Lincoln Hotel, where the businessman had booked a room
for him. It had gotten dark and cold. Ernie had a bite to
eat at a small restaurant on the street corner. He tried
to process the many impressions of the day. He simply
had to share them with someone. Quickly, he dialed the
phone number to reach Hedi in Switzerland. To her it all
sounded too good to be true. She asked quietly whether
it could all possibly be "pie in the sky."

Ernie himself had wondered if he were dreaming or
not. At the same time, he knew God could do wonderful
things. How often had he asked God to open doors in
America? How often had he traveled through the country
with film projectors and brochures, preaching and raising
funds in churches and halls? He'd been showered with
admiration and promises, and, more than once, left with
empty pockets! He did not lose faith that things could
turn around positively in the United States. He could
only hope for the best in this new acquaintanceship. Hedi
observed these developments much more soberly from a
healthy distance.

The next morning Ernie was right on time as he
stepped into one of the posh offices of the high rise. Mr.
Barbalo invited him in, handing him a telex from Mr.
Griffin. He would be unable to come to New York that
day–for health reasons! Not even thirty minutes had
passed until a secretary brought over another telex,
saying that the police had prevented Griffin from exiting
the country. He was due to appear in court and could
not leave Chile. Ernie was quite relieved at having been
spared from facing such an embarrassing meeting. The
atmosphere was congenial as they talked about how to
proceed with the BO 105. A charter contract would be

profitable for both sides. They decided to meet again and let everything go through their heads once more before coming to an agreement.

Two days later, the draft of the contract was read to Ernie. The secretary typed it up. Mr. Barbalo asked Ernie for his passport. He wanted to go see the notary public right away, whose office was just a few floors below. A short while later, Ernie held the notarized charter contract for his BO 105 in his hands. It was January 17, 1983. Now, Ernie was to go on to Chile to hand the machine over to a certain Mr. Garcia, who was Mr. Barbalo's representative there.

As Barbalo said good-bye, he laid it on Ernie's heart not to talk about the contract made with the state-owned oil company in Chile for the moment. The current company did not know their contract would not be renewed in May. Tired but happy, Ernie made the long journey home. He discussed the new situation at length with family and co-workers. Everyone hoped and prayed that their BO 105 would be in good hands.

Barbalo had promised Ernie to visit him in Trogen on February 23. Sickness, although nothing serious, prevented him from keeping his promise. The events to follow would bring more and more cloudy days to the skies over Salem. The wheels set in motion, however, could no longer be stopped.

Barbalo called. He explained that since the contract with the oil company would not start until May, he had signed an interim contract with the Marines in Chile. There was one condition: the helicopter would have to be registered in that country. Ernie would then have to have the HB-XHE deleted from the registry in Bern speedily. Barbalo had a pilot in Chile who was waiting for the job. To accomplish this in Bern, Ernie needed the paperwork of the chopper. He requested it from Chile; to his utter amazement, the papers were gone. Barbalo promised to inquire around. He found out that Baudrand, a former acquaintance of Ernie, was holding them. He promised to use a special messenger service to mail them to Ernie.

This gave Ernie time to make some inquiries for himself. He contacted the Marines, but no one knew anything about the contract. Ernie still could not believe Barbalo wanted to trick him. Yet, he didn't have a good feeling or any peace in his spirit about it. On one of his next trips to America, Ernie talked to Barbalo again. He recounts the conversation:

> Without beating around the bush, I told Barbalo that the Marines in Chile had had no clue about a contract with him. While I was speaking, I studied his face carefully. For a brief moment, he seemed embarrassed about my obvious doubts. Had I offended him? Had I gone too far? He said that he had signed the contract with a contractor working for the Marines. It could be that they personally had no knowledge of it. That was entirely possible, but it wasn't enough to dispel the dark clouds gathering on the horizon. On the inside, I became more and more indignant over this "temporary annulment" of our Swiss registration.
>
> "There is no such thing," I countered. "A machine is either registered or it is not. Where do you get your information?"
>
> I was surprised at my own critical tone of voice.
>
> He said his representative in Chile had given him these instructions to follow. This was usual business practice there, he assured me.
>
> He continued on persistently, "If we lose this deal, I'll have to sue you for breach of contract. My pilot has been in Chile for days, sitting at the beach. He must be paid."
>
> I was in dire straits. Barbalo's mask had fallen. A deep pain pierced my soul. It became clear to me that I had fallen into the hands of a trickster. The

pressure of all his scenarios, which came close to blackmail, made it hard for me to think straight any more. He presented a letter written to the Chilean Aviation Bureau. In it, I had promised to have the Swiss registration cancelled as soon as possible. It was written in Spanish, and Barbalo translated it word-for-word for me. If it were a trick, I could only hope I'd be able to discover it before it were too late. With this vague hope, I yielded to his pressure and signed the paper.

Back in Switzerland, Ernie sent a telex to the Chilean Aviation Bureau. He attempted to find out if it were possible to fly machines in Chile that were registered abroad. Later that night, Barbalo called from New York. Hedi was already in bed, and with pounding heart, listened to Ernie's side of the conversation. He was apologizing for something, which surprised her. What in the world did he have to apologize for? The discussion went on and on, getting more heated by the minute. It lasted until after midnight. She understood that Barbalo had learned about Ernie's inquiries at the aviation bureau. He was offended that Ernie didn't trust him and held him for no better than Griffin. In the end, Ernie was spelling something and writing at the same time. The tension in the air was tangible. Hedi got up, went down to Ernie and looked over his shoulder. What was he writing? Something Spanish? She didn't get it. She looked at her husband, her eyes full of question marks. Beads of sweat stood on his forehead. Finally, he hung up and let out a loud sigh.

"Hedi, he forced me to write a telegram and a telex to the Chilean Aviation Bureau. I'm supposed to say it was all a misunderstanding and that my last telex was irrelevant. Look at this—it's all in Spanish. I have to send the telegram immediately and have the telex sent tomorrow from St. Gallen. He threatened to get his attorneys on the case and sue me for a million dollars in damages."

It was a hard night for the Tanners. They talked about Barbalo at Helimission on a daily basis, even at the dinner table. Any hopes about a fair agreement with this strange man were dwindling. After about two and a half weeks, the helicopter documents finally arrived in Trogen by special courier. They were then sent to the Aviation Bureau in Bern which confirmed the cancellation of the registration of the HB-XHE to the Chilean bureau on March 29. Upon Ernie's inquiry, Barbalo said the machine was insured in Chile for 400,000 Swiss-Francs. Ernie could terminate his own insurance. He, Barbalo, would bring all the documents when he would come to Trogen as agreed on April 19. Instead of stopping the insurance, Ernie increased his premium to include hijacking.

Ernie's mind was racing. Being a Christian, he wanted to trust all people. However, he could not shake off fear due to the wheeling-dealing tactics of his mysterious counterpart. Day and night he pondered how to break out of this vicious cycle. Things came to a head when the Chilean Marines called to tell him that a certain Mr. Garcia was offering to sell them the BO 105. He had shown them a copy of the purchasing agreement signed by Ernie which said that Barbalo had paid for the chopper in cash. The commander of the Marines just wanted to call to say he didn't trust this Garcia.

This piece of news was a hard blow for Ernie. Yet, no matter how bad, the message showed him with whom he was dealing. It was hard for him to stay calm on the outside. His inner peace had been thrown out of balance. How could he serve God if hatred and anger kept rising up on the inside of him? How could he minister to others if he himself couldn't get these things under his feet?

Finally he decided to bury his destructive self-accusations. Silence was the only answer to his questions about God's intentions in this dark hour of testing. Only much, much later could he say he had learned several lessons: first, it takes practice to love your enemy and to forgive him. Secondly, brotherly love believes all things but has nothing to do with naivete. God had elevated Ernie into a responsible position, but he had blindly believed all people. He had not thought it possible that a person would not just steal an offering but also steal an entire helicopter paid for with offerings! The chopper was only bought to help serve people in need. Finally, maybe Barbalo had had to meet Ernie to comprehend how faithful and powerful God really is. The latter thought carried Ernie through those days and nights when things got really difficult.

Barbalo didn't show up again in Trogen on April 19, but no one was surprised. A telex sent by his secretary said that Barbalo was being delayed in Rio. It was received with an unbelieving smile. The telex stated further that Barbalo would be available in Paris on the weekend. He understood why Ernie was "frustrated." Ernie then traveled to Paris to suggest dissolving the contract. Barbalo couldn't be found anywhere. Shortly thereafter, Barbalo called and promised to come on May 3. If he didn't show up then, there was no need for Ernie to believe him any further. Of course, he didn't show up because of an "accident." An acquaintance in Santiago informed Ernie that Barbalo was trying by all means possible to register the BO in his name down in Chile.

Ernie, therefore, took steps to try to register the BO in Switzerland again. For this purpose he needed a document issued in Chile certifying the helicopter's operability. On May 27th he flew there, sought out an attorney and went to speak with the commander of the Marines.

Chapter 34

The End of Charlie

Once again, Hedi's work was disrupted by the harsh ringing of the telephone. These days she did not consider it a friend. That loud thing had brought them too much unpleasant news. She allowed it to ring a few times before picking it up. The noise in the receiver told her it was a call from abroad. Fortunately, it was Joel Barker calling from Kenya. She understood his English very well; he always spoke slowly and clearly.

"Hello, Joel. How are you?"

"I'm fine, thank God. But I had an accident this afternoon."

"Excuse me? You mean, with the helicopter?"

"Yes, with the helicopter. It was destroyed, and Rick is dead."

Hedi drew in a quick breath. She didn't know what to say. Joel fell silent as well.

"Did you get hurt? Are you well?" she asked, very disturbed.

"Yes, I am. It's a miracle."

He told her what had happened. They had spent all day flying sand from the river to the mission station. It had been quite a chore, and they had taken turns flying. He, Joel, had flown back to the river to pick up empty kerosene tanks. Rick had loaded them into a net and hooked it onto the chopper. The machine had then slowly turned over on its side. He had been unable to pull it up again. A terrible bang ensued as the main rotor hit the ground and broke in pieces. The helicopter simply remained lying on its side. He had turned off the engine and gotten out through the upper hatch. A few steps away lay Rick face down. He was dead.

Hedi started to cry. It took all her concentration to stay on the line. She kept asking him, "Did you get hurt? Are you well?" Then she got a grip on herself. They briefly discussed what needed be done and who needed to be informed: the aviation bureau, the insurance company, Ernie in America, Rick's parents. Joel would do what needed to be done in Kenya.

Hedi put down the receiver. Lukas was standing next to her. Both sat down on the floor and started to cry. It was already evening, so the aviation bureau and insurance office were closed.

"If only Daddy were here," Lucky said. "Can't you call him?"

"No, he is on the go, and I don't know where he'll be tonight. Come on, let's pray for him to call us. Sometimes, he does."

The praying and waiting paid off. It was already quite late but Ernie did call. Hedi didn't know how to tell him the bad news. He noticed her hesitation and immediately thought Barbalo had launched another attack.

"No, we haven't heard from Barbalo," Hedi assured him. "But I have bad news from Kenya."

Slowly, she told him all she knew. Ernie couldn't fathom how such a terrible accident could possibly have happened. He kept asking over and over again, but Hedi had no answers.

"It's still the middle of the day here. I'll try to reach Rick's parents. God will have to help me comfort them. Please pray for me."

Ernie and Hedi tried to comfort each other, but it wasn't easy. Both had to cope with the disaster by themselves.

Slowly, more news trickled in from Kenya. Joel had informed the police. They sent two guards to watch over the helicopter. A doctor had filled out Rick's death certificate. Upon his parents' request, his body was flown back to America via the embassy.

A storm caused the river to swell. The helicopter was lying at its banks. To prevent the machine from being washed away, the police tied it to a tree. They took their job as guards very seriously. They were so stubborn that they didn't even allow Joel to get the helicopter out of the water. The fuselage was being tossed to and fro, rubbing on the rocks. Whatever could have been saved of the chopper was now totally destroyed by the water. When Ernie took a look at the wreck a month later, his heart was deeply saddened. Good old Charlie! It had served him in so many invaluable ways! And now it was gone!

Later, Joel reported how he had found comfort right after the disaster. Deeply shaken, he had walked along the river. A deep sense of loss and loneliness had overtaken him. He wondered if he himself were still alive. Yes, he was alive. He was breathing. He was walking. He could see. He could think! It had to have been a miracle. Angels had protected him so that not even a hair on his head had been touched. And those very same angels had ushered Rick right into the presence of Jesus. Gradually, this thought had quieted his feelings down. It brought peace into the tumult raging in his heart.

Chapter 35

Odyssey of the XLL

In 1982, Helimission had three helicopters on the mission field: Charlie in Kenya, Yankee in Cameroon and the BO in Chile. Just like the needs, the circle of friends of Helimission had thankfully also expanded. Both the large and the small bills which came in the mail every day could be paid off through the office in Trogen. Ernie stood in awe, thanking God continuously. Although Helimission didn't have a surplus, even the larger invoices were always paid in full.

"It was just enough," Ernie used to say often and would remember Fanny's dream.

In the fall he received a call from the Philippines. That country with its many thousands of islands could really use a helicopter. Ernie traveled to Manila and spent some time with various missionaries. He grew to love the Filipinos, who in spite of the bitter poverty they faced, always smiled. It didn't take long for him to envision the manifold possibilities of using a helicopter there.

Back in Switzerland, someone offered him a slightly used machine in top condition. He grabbed this opportunity that he saw coming from the hand of God. It would take a few months until the helicopter would be ready for use. Its dedication was scheduled for the spring of '83. As part of a large crusade, the blue-and-red XLL gave sightseeing tours. Afterward, it was dedicated in prayer to spreading the Gospel in the Third World. A large crowd of Christians had come. Preachers from all kinds of independent churches in St. Gallen gathered to join in prayer. Thereafter, the XLL stayed in Belp for a little while. It was then fitted with important peripheral equipment, such as floating devices–inflatable balloons on the landing gear–and a radio. Finally, it was packed up into a container and left Genoa for Manila by boat. It arrived on September 2, shortly before its pilot came over in mid-September.

Right from the beginning in the port of Manila, the XXL faced difficulties. This was the first time Ernie had brought a helicopter into another country as "freight." Hitherto, he had always flown the machines in. His experiences with customs and the government had always been positive. This time the customs officers sealed up the container and imposed an import tax upon it, which amounted to half of the chopper's value. Despite all promises made by Marcos' government, the machine could not be imported free of customs. It just sat there in its container. Several missions organizations applied for a customs exemption. They appealed to the head of government. They received appointments for meetings and were promised that the papers would be signed. Because of this, Ernie flew to the Philippines himself several times. Meanwhile, time also flew by. The pilot returned to America.

All of this was happening in the year that Barbalo had stolen their beautiful BO 105 and after Charlie had crashed. Of their four helicopters, only one was still flying—the machine in Cameroon.

One day Hedi observed her husband sad and lost in thought. The look in her eyes clearly formed the question: should we continue or give up? Slowly Ernie stood up, his back, erect.

"Hedi, I know. I know what you're thinking. But—by God's grace—the helicopters will fly again. We may have lost the battle this time, but we shall win the war!"

Although Hedi had to let out a deep sigh, she had gotten her answer. Ernie's old fire hadn't gone out. The devil had hit him hard, but Ernie was ready to fight back.

In May 1984, Ernie Tanner wrote to his many friends in Switzerland:

From February 5 - March 27, I kept seeking permission from President Marcos of the Philippines to import the helicopter without paying customs. Since I had never received a negative answer in all of this time of waiting, I did not lose my patience and kept hoping and praying. Of course, I visited members of Parliament, spoke to other government officers and wrote letters as well. During all of those weeks, I had countless opportunities to serve God. I was determined to preach the Gospel, with or without a helicopter. There were many open doors. We visited Bible studies and prayer groups in hospitals, large offices, public buildings and town squares. People meet spontaneously–during their lunch breaks or after work–to praise and worship God. Many of these groups, some larger and some smaller, invited me to join them. One Sunday I spoke at a large square where about 7,000 mostly young people had gathered together. They met there every week, sat on the ground or simply stood there in the heat, enjoying their fellowship with God and with one another. I was allowed to show a short film about Helimission in a detention center. I also got permission to speak to the inmates two times after that. As a result of all of these positive experiences, I have been greatly strengthened and encouraged in my inner man.

All efforts seemed futile, but Ernie came up with a new plan. The container was loaded back onto a ship and taken to the American island of Guam, about 625 miles east of where they were in the Pacific Ocean. Importing it was no problem at all. The helicopter was reassembled. In August 1984, Ernie carried out a test flight. The machine flew excellently. He prepared it for a longer flight into the Philippines–all the way across the water. For the customs office, there is a tremendous difference between importing a helicopter and flying it into the country.

"Man thinks, and God directs," the saying goes.

At the beginning of 1985, the door to Ethiopia suddenly opened up again quite unexpectedly. A great famine struck, and God used the situation to His advantage. The nation and its government were crying out for help. After communicating with the mission stations in the Philippines, everyone agreed that the plight of the Ethiopians should receive priority. Both heavy and joyful in heart, the Filipinos released their XLL to help feed the starving Ethiopians.

It took two trips per ship before the machine would reach its destination on the other side of the world. In March 1985, it arrived at the port of Assab on the Red Sea. Duly prepared with all the necessary documents and permits, Ernie was able to take it into his possession and load it on to a truck headed for Addis Ababa. It was a hot and tiring two-day transfer. The chopper then served in the area north of the capital city for a good two years. It flew into refugee camps, transporting government officials and members of the Peace Corps to their destinations. In February 1987, however, an accident put it out of commission. The five men on board were fortunate in this crash. They were able to leave the machine, lying on its side, unscathed.

▲ ▲
The Tanner family in front of their fireplace.
(Ch. 32)
▲
Jack and Ernie in Winterthur. (Ch. 1)

▲ ▲
Summer camp in Bad Duerrheim. Here, Ernie
painted the picture and kissed Hedi while holding
up a chair. (Ch. 3)
▲
The house surrounded by nature. To the left is the
office of Helimission. (Ch. 4)

▲ ▲
Piper training in Altenrhein. (Ch. 9)
▲
Refueling the chopper on the desert border of
Insgeam between Algeria and Niger during their
first flight over in 1971. (Ch. 14)

▲
Preaching at a stop along the Gorilla Path. (Ch. 7)

►
On the "Gorilla Path." (Ch. 7)

▲ ▲
Mpane: Carriers at the end of their journey. (Ch. 7)
▲
The three women who wanted to know whether
Jesus had already come back. (Ch. 7)

▲ ▲
The water pump developed by Ernie Tanner; six of
them were installed. One of them provided drinking
water for ten months to the German Arabati camp
in the Danakil desert. (Ch. 23)

▲
Ernie Tanner on the morning after the attack.
(Ch. 26)

▲ ▲
A tribal chief and his medicine man in Betshatti in
the jungle of Cameroon next to our first helicopter.
(Ch. 13)

▲
A strategy meeting in Bulki, Ethiopia, with Lloyd
Stinson, SIM. (Ch. 24)

▲
Part of the twelve tons of special flour consisting of wheat, soy, and milk powder, donated by the Swiss Red Cross for Ethiopia. (Ch. 23)

▶
The XCX being loaded into the DC-7. (Ch. 23).

▲
Ethiopia: The
ministry of
Samaritans.

◄
The wages of
a preacher: a
crocodile.

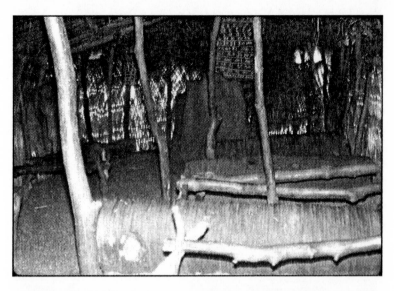

▲ ▲
The "comfortable" seats of a bush church. (Ch. 18)
▲
Bush village. An ideal "airstrip." A jungle village in
southwest Cameroon. (Ch. 18)

▲
House and hangar
in Bamenda.
(Ch. 18)

◄
A water tank
is hoisted onto
its pedestal.
Cameroon 1984.
(Ch. 18)

▲ ▲
The first helicopter on the mission field. (Ch. 18)
▲
Preaching to the Pokot tribe. (Kenya)

▲
Packing
Christmas gifts
for Italy in
"assembly line"
fashion. (Ch. 32)

◄
Earthquake in
Italy. (Ch. 32)

▲
A gift is well-received. (Ch. 32).

▲ ▲
The XLL after the accident. (Ch. 35)
▲
The house in Zaire. (Ch. 39)

▲ ▲
The hangar in Zaire. (Ch. 39)
▲
Dropping off corn sacks at a low altitude. (Ch. 42)

▲

Famine in Ethiopia. (Ch. 42)

▲
Hosts of
people
gather up
corn.
(Ch. 42)

▶
The Tukana
tribe.

◄
The Coma tribe.

◄
The Pokot tribe
(in Kenya).

▲ ▲
A Mursi woman in Ethiopia.
▲
Safety Seminar in February 1988.

234

HB – XDK: 1971 – 1975

HB – XCX:　　1972 – 1983

HB – XLL:　　1983 –

HB – XPN:　　1985 –

HB – XSH:　　1987 –

HB – YDY:　　1976 –

HB – XHE:　　1978 – 1983

HB – XON:　　1983 –

HB – XRH:　　1986 – 1987

N1105W:　　1988 –

Chapter 36
"What Else Can I Do For You?"

The atmosphere at Salem, both the house and the office, was laden with both excitement and anxiety. Mr. T. Wilson of London had announced his arrival that afternoon. A true gentleman, this insurance broker always came wearing fine perfume and dressed to the teeth, tie and all. All of the helicopters had comprehensive and liability insurance under his company, Lloyds. Mr. Wilson was no stranger to Trogen, but nonetheless, his visits always caused a lot of hustle and bustle. Hedi was trying to decide which tea she would offer him. The secretaries were blowing dust off of their desks and stacking up their files neatly. They prepared the insurance papers, receipts and helicopter documents for his perusal. They also made sure the large Helimission office was immaculate.

The tenor of Ernie's talks with T. Wilson was friendly. The two negotiated new conditions for 1984. At the conclusion, Wilson asked, "Do you have any other questions, or is there anything else I can do for you?" It might have been a routine question asked out of politeness, but Wilson seemed genuine. Ernie looked at Hedi briefly, an inquiring look on his face. She nodded discreetly.

Ernie opened up completely to the surprised insurance agent. He told him the entire tragic story about the BO 105. Since that time, Ernie had been unable to get a new Swiss license for the machine. All the odds seemed to be against him. The greatest hindrance was the large distance between Switzerland and Chile. Then, it was hard to pin down Barbalo who was traveling all over, and yet was nowhere to be found. Precious time had passed. Barbalo used circumstances to his advantage to constantly think up new games. Numerous telex messages had gone back and forth. New contacts in Santiago were informed.

The Chilean attorney tried to get hold of the vital document certifying the helicopter's operability. Meanwhile a customs problem had arisen. Even the Swiss embassy was involved, without success, up until now. Barbalo had cajoled Ernie into coming to a meeting with the attorney in Chile on August 11. Barbalo himself didn't even show up. His excuse was that he was upset about a fist fight between his representative, Garcia, and Ernie's representative, Sam. In September, the helicopter was confiscated by Chilean customs as ordered by the Chilean Aviation Bureau. At the same time, the Bureau confirmed that Barbalo was the owner of the machine. It was up to Ernie to prove that Helimission was the rightful owner. This would only be possible if the BO were registered in Switzerland again. It was enough to drive anyone to despair.

Mr. Wilson could not understand why the Swiss Aviation Bureau could not register the machine again.

"I went to Bern to talk to those people myself," Ernie said with resignation. "Barbalo had, through an attorney in Geneva, sent photocopies of the counterfeit purchase contract to the aviation people, who accepted them as genuine."

While Ernie continued the story, Mr. Wilson listened very, very carefully. The customs issue in Chile couldn't be wished away. The customs office was threatening to auction off the helicopter. In November, Ernie had even received an invoice from them—not for duty, but as a penalty—which was higher than the value of the bird.

"Two weeks ago when I was not at home, Barbalo spoke with my wife on the telephone saying that he had sent us a letter. He said he was an honest man and wanted to meet with me in order to find a solution to the problem. He even called again a couple of days ago—again while I wasn't there. Interesting, isn't it?" Ernie closed thoughtfully.

A call interrupted their talk. Ernie came back infuriated and sat down again.

"The aviation bureau just told me that a notary public and the Swiss embassy in New York have confirmed that the notarization of the purchasing contract was all right and the contract is for real. So they can't register the helicopter."

Lines appeared on Mr. Wilson's forehead.

"Don't take that sitting down, Mr. Tanner. I know an attorney in Zurich who's a pro on aviation issues. Get in touch with him. Remember, you are insured against any kind of loss, including theft. I'm going to report this case. This is the first time I've ever heard of such a thing, by the way."

Mr. Wilson gathered up the paperwork and put it into his briefcase. As they were parting, he repeated his friendly offer, "Is there anything else I can do for you, Mr. Tanner?"

"Yes, Mr. Wilson, pray," Ernie replied.

December 5 brought another turning point to this unique story. The insurance company had commissioned Beaumont & Son in London to look into the case. Beaumont & Son was responsible for dealing with legal questions in the cases of accidents where Lloyds must pay. They had attorneys all over the world. Particularly known to the Helimission were those law offices found in Santiago, New York, Paris and London. Now those experts in law began spinning a web of letters, telexes and phone calls to make things tight for Barbalo. Then, he retaliated.

In April of 1984, Ernie found a letter in his mailbox. It stated he must come to a court hearing in Paris: Barbalo was suing Ernie Tanner for slander. The document said Ernie had until June to choose a representative.

The letter was forwarded to England.

Chapter 37

Half-a-Dozen

Ernie was trying to decide how to replace the XCX, which had been destroyed in Kenya. In the past, a French machine, the "Ecureuil," which means "squirrel," had been recommended to him by several people. It was a fast and powerful whirlybird. He was thinking about using it in Cameroon. There was a French company in the port city of Douala able to maintain the chopper, and that would be an asset. It would save Swiss mechanics from having to fly to Cameroon for every 100-hour checkup. The Yankee (XDY), which on the outside was very similar to the machine which had crashed, would make a good choice for Kenya.

In November 1983, the machine was ready. Its paint job was striking. It featured five dark-red stripes of varying widths right across its belly which got thinner leading up to its round red nose. Hedi found the nose amusing, which Ernie could not dispute.

Overjoyed, he wrote to his friends about it:

> We've received another miracle of God! Our newest machine, the HB-XON, is faster, more powerful and more comfortable than the Jet Ranger. Logging only 130 flight hours, it is practically new. Bud Spencer, the famous actor, was its former owner. Joel and I shall fly it to Cameroon in January. It will be the ninth time I will be crossing the Sahara Desert. I sincerely covet your prayers.

The office staff could tell plenty of stories about the excitement that accompanies buying a helicopter. Sylvia, who had gone through quite a few stressful periods with Hedi and Ernie, wrote about it:

I've been working for Helimission for five and a half years now. During that time, I've weathered a good number of storms and gone through calamities with the ministry. Every time I would approach my wits' end, though, I would witness the intervention of the Lord. At first, I was the only one working with Hedi and Ernie Tanner. As the Heli-fleet grew and the administrative tasks did too, the Lord increased our staff. It is a privilege for me to be able to work for the kingdom of God so directly even if I'm not on the front lines. For this, I am grateful to the Lord Jesus.

Sylvia was right. The Heli-fleet had grown–in spite of failures. Who would have thought that Ernie's wish for half-a-dozen machines would already come to pass in their eleventh year? Although two had "perished in battle" and a third was not "fit to fight," Helimission had obtained many victories. Wherever it went, it was always put to use in two ways–spiritually and materially. As a result, thousands of people in Cameroon, Bolivia, Kenya and Ethiopia had heard the joyful and liberating Gospel for the very first time. For shorter missions, the Cameroonian helicopter had gone to Zaire and to Nigeria. The pilots were reporting how God had given His blessing in spreading the Good News. It was a pleasure for them to be able to participate.

It is late afternoon on September 12, 1985. The long-awaited sound of the long-expected machine fills the air. Ernie Tanner lands the new helicopter, HB-XPN, in Trogen. It is the second "squirrel" and has been earmarked for a rescue mission in the Sudan. They only have one day to prepare for the long flight. The carpet must be replaced with waterproof material. An extra tank must be built in as well. All of the baggage is carefully weighed and loaded into the helicopter, piece by piece. The last few express parcels arrive at the post office in Trogen. The most important one, documents from the

Bern Aviation Bureau, comes in at 5 p.m. At 5:55 p.m., the chopper takes off from the small heliport. The skies are as clear as they can be. Ernie Tanner circles around and then heads off for Samaden.

Saturday, September 14. Takeoff in Samaden. Heavily loaded, the helicopter takes on the Bernina mountain pass headed for Italy. Refueling at Bari. Landing on the island of Korfu, Greece, at 4 p.m. Calling Trogen: everything is fine!

Sunday, September 15. Flying to Crete over many islands and the mountains of Peloponnesus at a height of 13,000 feet. Refueling in Herakleion. For two hours and twenty minutes, nothing but sky and water. The Egyptian coast becomes visible. Good landing in Alexandria. Calling Trogen: everything is A-OK! The leased rescue boat and the lifejackets are being sent back to Switzerland.

Monday, September 16. Flight along the green Nile River across Egypt with backwinds at 3,300 feet. It is getting hot–Africa. Landing in Assuan at 2:20 p.m.

Tuesday, September 17. Continuing their flight, Ernie crosses the Assuan Reservoir, the border to the Sudan; the Nubian desert; and, at Abu Hamed, catches up with the Nile River again. Shortly after midday, he lands in Khartoum. He is welcomed by a representative of the UN Refugee Agency. Unfortunately, it takes another five days until five official bodies grant them their flight permit. Only then can they go ahead and help those in need.

El Genina is a small desert village close to the border of Chad. It seems to all of a sudden be waking up out of its millennium slumber. One has to ask: how can people possibly live there in the center of Africa, surrounded by thousands of square miles of desert? In the northern district of Darfur, to which El Genina belongs, about 300,000 people live in extreme poverty. This year, there was insufficient rainfall.

For months, refugees from Chad have been arriving. These 120,000 people add to the problems of the already starving population. By now, most are little more than skin and bones. All of these desperate people huddle together in the villages. Representatives of the UN and other organizations rush in to help their forlorn fellow human beings. The small Swiss helicopter is sponsored by the UN as well. Also an Ecureuil, it is the same type as in Cameroon but with blue and red stripes. Food and supplies are being delivered daily on giant transport planes. The chopper's task is to take the rations on to the villages and refugee camps. Ernie is once again eyewitness to the horrors suffered by a sector of humanity. He sees extreme suffering, much grief, many tears.

Within a matter of three weeks, the Beda refugee camp has grown from 6,000 to 12,000 people. A young French doctor and two nurses are doing all they can to care for them. A sick bay, latrines and storage units have to be set up. An American-led aid campaign uses Chinook helicopters to fly in supplies. Ernie transports personnel and medicine to them there.

As though the suffering were not enough, cholera breaks out and spreads. Isolated quarters, trained personnel, infusion equipment, buckets, special beds... everything is needed.

It is not exactly an ideal start for new missionaries. Nevertheless, right there in El Genina–at the end of the world–Dean, a new Helimission pilot from New Zealand, begins his time of service. His young wife Kaylene and their one-year-old son Daniel join him. He chooses to stay in it for the long haul, working diligently and suffering compassionately along with the hurting.

Chapter 38

The Children Sprout Wings

My, how time flies! Helimission has been in existence for more than ten years; yet no one has time to celebrate. At the Tanner house, there is a steady coming and going, not only of guests, but of family members as well. Before each of the young family members leaves the nest, Ernie has them write something for his newsletter. He is well aware that not just Hedi and he had sacrificed for the ministry, but that the children had also, involuntarily, contributed a great deal as well. The first-born son, of course, got to start things off:

Being the oldest of the Tanner children, I had the opportunity of following my parents' vision from the very beginning. I got to experience a lot firsthand. Our "home, sweet home" housed many visitors, which meant it was never boring. The mission took its toll on our family life because our father was gone so much. During my childhood, the children's summer camps and youth retreats made a significant impact on me. So did listening to my father during his speaking engagements. I also had an accident which I only survived by a miracle of God.

While doing my professional training, I went through a time of diverse personal conflicts. I distanced myself from my family, and our relationship became cool. I have to say that my own personality was strengthened during this difficult phase of my life. I have a new job as a technician at IBM, Switzerland, where I can continue to develop professionally in years to come. In February 1983, I attended military training for recruits. I was recommended for further training to become a corporal, i.e. a group leader. I'll finish up in September. I'd like to go to school to become an officer although I'm working at IBM currently. At this point in time, I am not yet sure when my path will lead me to join in my father's work.

Immanuel

The oldest daughter was the next to write:

"That ye may show forth the excellencies of Him who called you out of darkness into His marvelous light" (1 Peter 2:9). It's already been six years since my conversion. I can testify that life with Jesus is exciting. My own life has been accompanied by many small miracles. I have been working as a practical nurse for two and a half years, and now I am training to become an RN. I'm also involved with the youth of the Buchegg church in Zurich. There are so many possibilities to share the love of God, whether with patients, colleagues or fellow students. The people around me are searching for the truth. I sense a longing for peace in their hearts. This challenges me daily to really live the Christian walk. I am grateful to my heavenly Father for His goodness in leading me to this particular school. I know He is preparing me for future ministry, wherever that may be.

Miriam

Her one-year-younger sister had this to share:

Born in 1962, I didn't know that, one day, I would be the middle child of five siblings. I have to say I had neither great advantages nor disadvantages as a result of that. When I was finished with school, though, I didn't have the slightest idea as to what I wanted to do. I had to go through a time of testing, particularly in my patience. It wasn't easy for me to know the will of God. It was during that time that I really felt my parents' encouragement by word and deed like never before. I shall forever be grateful to them for that. By God's grace and His faithfulness, I have become a physician's assistant. It's a job which gives me a lot of satisfaction. It is currently my desire to serve my heavenly Father in this way. I'm not sure, yet, whether my training will take me to the mission field or elsewhere. I'll see. At the moment, I am still working as a PA. Now and then, I tell the Lord, "Please teach me patience–and teach me now!"

Damaris

Next in line was the second-oldest son. He wrote a short but honest appraisal:

I was born in Trogen in 1965. Currently, I'm in my third year as an apprentice in precision mechanics at a company called Wild in Heerbrugg. I drive everyday to the Rhine River Valley with my little motorbike. It takes about forty minutes. At night, I get home tired and often half-frozen. My bike usually needs fixing up in the evenings–it's become a bit of a hobby by now. I like Helimission most of the time. Sometimes, I don't, especially when the problems and responsibilities seem to be overtaxing my dad. Still, I actually want to help him in future. My long-term goal is to work as a helicopter mechanic.

Simon

Last but not least, the youngest child was also given the chance to say something:

I have a wish that can never be fulfilled: I wish I'd been born a few years earlier; that way, I wouldn't have to go to school for so long. I'd be nearly grown up already and able to help Daddy in his terrific work. Since I was only born in Trogen in '70, I've got to bite the bullet and keep going to school a few more years. I think I'm doing my mom a great favor by making her life a bit more exciting. When all of my brothers and sisters have flown the coop, I'll still be here at the "Go-and-get-it-Club". Either I rake leaves or mend electric plugs. I start the oven or buy bread or clean up the basement or whatever. Oh, well, I guess that's what the youngest are there for.

Lucky

Chapter 39

Zaire

Ernie and Mr. Riddle of the Baptist mission in Zaire had been in touch for quite some time. The missionary had often asked for help involving a helicopter. After a while, a plan began coming together for a three-week mission. Ernie himself flew the machine from Cameroon via Gabon to Kinshasa. He landed to find everything well-prepared. During the thirty flying hours which ensued, much was put in motion for the kingdom of God. Norman Riddle described how the mission was carried out:

> In one village, I asked whether there were men who had become Christians when an evangelist had preached in their area years ago. Had any not returned to sorcery but remained faithful to God and stayed with only one wife? There were a few. We made two of them deacons, and two women, deaconesses. We had an ordination service where we lay hands and blessed them as leaders among the Christians. One of them became an overseer, who would read the Word of God to them. Unfortunately, we were unable to send them a Bible teacher, but we encouraged them to share the Gospel of Christ in the surrounding villages. Between November 4th-19th, then, we visited one hundred and nineteen villages. We were able to reach more than 10,000 people. We also finished building three airstrips. There were eleven chiefs among the 2,970 converts. In seventy-nine places, the villagers were asking for a Bible teacher to come. But we don't have enough of them to go around.

Norman Riddle closed his letter with an earnest appeal for prayer for more Bible teachers. He also stated clearly that the mission wouldn't have accomplished all of the above without the helicopter's aid. Of course, it is not hard to see how a chopper can greatly alleviate material, physical need; less obvious is how vital one can be in bringing spiritual life as well. The Word of God teaches us not to neglect either aspect. Only eternity will tell how important both sides were to God. This is the philosophy which drives Helimission.

Chapter 40

The Mysterious Gas of Nyos

As soon as pilot Dean heard of disaster striking a bush village, it was second nature for him to turn around and head for Nyos, Cameroon. He wrote this in his monthly report:

It is August 23 at 7:15 a.m. I take off to bring a team of doctors to Badji. The village is quite isolated and lies in the northeastern sector of the country. The team wants nothing more than to make its routine rounds in the bush hospitals. The Katsina Valley, which we have to fly through, is covered in thick clouds. We land on a small soccer field to wait for them to dissipate. Coincidentally, we meet a teacher who tells us appalling news about Nyos. We must admit the "bush telephone" functions incredibly well! Immediately, I go visit the local police chief. I offer him Helimission's help. Nobody seems to be grasping how serious the situation is but no one seems to be prepared to accompany me there either—for fear of some "gas." I decide to fly there by myself.

The first thing I notice is the lake. It looks horrendous. It used to be a beautiful dark blue color, encompassed by mountains to the north. Now, it looks like a dying pond with reddish-brown and black spots. On the surface float moldy plants. The steep cliff on the western side of the crater appears white instead of the usual black. On the shallow shore of the southern side, I notice plants and shrubs that look like they've been flattened by a huge wave. The once bubbly waterfall which, before, had been flowing cheerily into the lake is now silent. Dead animals lie at the foot of the hills. Particularly, the bloated carcasses of sheep catch my eye. The sight is indescribable...terrible.

As I fly over the village, I begin to comprehend the true dimensions of the disaster. Hundreds of dead bodies greet me. I ask Jesus for wisdom and strength. Then, I decide to land and check things out. A Catholic priest from Wum has just arrived minutes before I do. Together, we walk through the village. Dead bodies are everywhere. The stench of decaying flesh penetrates our noses. Whatever type of gas it had been, it had sped up the decomposition process, particularly in adult bodies. The people simply remained where they had taken their last breath.

Strangely enough, there is no sign of fear or panic. Some lie in their beds; others, on the floor by their beds. Families are discovered lying close together. Some had fallen into their fireplaces. One poor woman was even overwhelmed by the gas as she was giving birth. Life seems to have just been snuffed out here. Then, we meet six villagers who, for some incredible reason, have survived the ordeal!

The following day, Steve, a second pilot, joins Dean in returning to the area. He writes a few of his impressions:

On August 24, Dean and I fly back into the disaster area with ninety-five liters of water on board. We distribute it and help where we can. We witness the last few funerals taking place. We fly on to Subum where we learn that about four of every ten persons have died. We meet doctors who have come over from the capital. We must evacuate eight seriously injured people to the hospital in Wum. On Thursday, we fly a CNN team to the Nyos area. We also fly journalists to Wum, where there are many survivors. On Saturday, the Swiss rescue team flies with us. The day is declared an official "Day of Mourning" in Cameroon. All of the stores are closed. Neither playing music nor dancing is allowed. Only church music can be sung or played. We are impressed by the sincerity of compassion toward the fate of the survivors.

Chapter 41

Two Versus One

"Here's the train connection you wanted."

Ruth, Ernie's young, hard-working secretary, placed a note with the times on his desk. He looked at it briefly: departing Lausanne June 2 at 7:38 a.m., arriving in Paris at 11:28 a.m.

"What time does the meeting start?" he asked, somewhat absent-mindedly.

"At three. You'll have enough time to catch lunch before that."

"I don't think I'll feel like eating, but I'm glad to arrive early enough to get my act together. Who knows what's awaiting me in Paris?"

It had not yet come to a legal hearing, but Ernie could still feel the pressure rising as the date drew closer. While he traveled through the French landscape, he went through his files one more time. This was about Barbalo. Ernie was hoping this story would finally come to an end. The actual hearing would have to take place in a Parisian court because Barbalo was French. Now everything was dependent upon the graphologists, who would also be coming to Paris that day. Would they determine Ernie's signature on the disputed purchase contract to be real or bogus? Ernie knew it was a fake; he did not know if the experts could ascertain that. What if they couldn't? Ernie didn't dare to think of the implications: Helimission would die. Fortunately, it was not Ernie Tanner's mission! No, it was God's.

Ernie's thoughts moved faster than the TGV express train he was riding. In Paris, an industrious lawyer would be expecting him. He worked for Beaumont & Son, who, in turn, received backing from the Lloyds insurance company. Having them behind him was a good feeling, like a thick and mighty wall of protection which Barbalo would have to run up against.

A cab took him to Avenue Aubriot where the office of the experts was located. There he met with Maître LeFevre, his lawyer. Together, they said hello to the three graphologists already there. Another gentleman was also introduced, and then the meeting started. Then the doors opened up one more time. A finely dressed gentleman appeared, nodded briefly, and sat down on the remaining empty chair. Ernie felt his face go hot. It was Barbalo! Nobody had indicated that his combatant would show up. He had to fight rising emotions. He concentrated on the conversation and its significance. He was surprised to realize there was no hatred in his heart toward Barbalo. It was a change that only God could have worked in him.

Finally, the corpus delicti, i.e. the original of the disputed contract, was pulled out from a stack of files. It was then handed over to the experts. In Spanish, it read that Ernie Tanner had sold the BO and had received the purchase price in cash. In the conversations with Barbalo, he had never discussed selling but only leasing it to him. The contract Ernie had signed in New York had been a charter contract.

Even though three years had gone by, Ernie remembered those hours very well. They had been the start of three years of worrying, hoping, fighting. He could truly say he tried everything from "A to Z," traveling to Chile, the States, London and now Paris. He wondered how long this would carry on—and how long his strength would hold out.

His mind was full of questions as he looked around. He tried to read the faces of the experts and make out what they were saying. He listened to the remarks of Maître LeFevre who was interrupted several times by Barbalo's lawyer. In the end, they agreed that the examination results would be sent to the lawyer via the court.

As they said goodbye, Maître LeFevre gave Ernie an encouraging look.

"Just be patient," he said.

"I've been trying to for many years now. What do you think? How long will it take for the results?"

"Maybe by the time winter comes...."

Winter did come. On December 1, Ernie received a letter from Beaumont & Son with forty-nine pages attached to it. He could make neither heads nor tails of the file. He looked at the letter, and his heart began beating faster. It read as follows:

> We seem to have made some progress in the French proceedings. I'm attaching the copy of the report submitted by the three experts commissioned by the court. The document is very technical. Two of the experts say your signature on the "Contrato di Compra Venta" is not authentic. The third does not see any evidence why it should not be genuine.
>
> Best regards,
> D.A.K.

Two versus one. Ernie could hardly believe it. He regained hope, noticing relief physically flooding into his body. He was almost looking forward to the day at court and to the final decision. But how long would it take now?

Chapter 42

Good News and Bad News

The year came to an end. Helimission was operating in four countries in Africa. Four dedicated pilots had done a marvelous job.

Ernie bought a fifth machine in Abu Dhabi, United Arab Emirates, at an incredibly good price. His first flight with it was to Uganda via Bahrain, Riad, Jedda, Sana, Addis Ababa and Nairobi. There, the helicopter was made ready for use in Africa. Almost new and with top instruments, it bore the Swiss registration number HB-XRH. Ernie described the bird to his family: it was beautifully painted in rainbow colors. Everyone who saw it liked it right off the bat.

Ernie had to wait for a flight permit in Uganda. It was there that very bad news from Trogen reached him. The XLL had crashed on a mountain slope in Ethiopia; it had been completely smashed against the cliffs. Its pilot Carson and his four passengers had miraculously been able to escape the machine in one piece. The news brought great sadness in Trogen and wherever else Helimission was active. Hedi was very grateful that those lives had been spared. Still, she was brokenhearted about the loss of the Jet Ranger XLL. That chopper had had a special place in her heart. She could hardly believe it was a total wreck.

Only three weeks after the disaster, Ernie returned home. Uganda had not granted him a flight permit. He came just in time for another piece of bad news. Steve, the pilot in Cameroon, had a three-year-old son, Colby. The boy was poisoned to death after drinking some disinfectant. All of them mourned and empathized with the grieving parents. The Helimission base in Bamenda now was home to a child's grave. The Bible verse, "Those who sow in tears. . . shall reap with joy," was a great comfort at this time.

On March 18, 1987, the strange chapter in their lives involving Fernando Rios Selvo de Barbalo–which had been pretty incomprehensible to all of them–came to an end. It wasn't a happy one for all involved. Due to falsification of the document concerning the BO 105, the court sentenced Barbalo to a symbolic penalty of one Swiss-Franc to be paid to Ernie as compensation for moral damage caused by his actions. Ernie received the verdict in writing. For days, he could not stop thinking, "Barbalo was brought to justice; God has vindicated me."

The Lloyds insurance company had gone into the proceedings against its own interests and then won. So it ended up paying for the helicopter which had been insured for theft. Never before in the history of Lloyds had something been stolen so treacherously. Mr. T. Wilson, the helpful British insurance agent, delivered the check to Trogen personally. He was invited to join everyone for a lovely fondue dinner. After all, it was time to celebrate that things had come to a positive close.

Chapter 43

Two Birthdays, One Trip

How often had Ernie shared anecdote after anecdote about Africa with Hedi! He knew just how to cast an impressive light on the continent. How often had he sighed, "You really must experience it for yourself one day!" How often had he longed for her to be at his side there! It would be of great benefit, for she would be able to understand his work all the better and to support him that much more.

Nineteen eighty-seven was a special year for both Ernie and Hedi: both were turning sixty years old! What could be a more fitting birthday gift than a trip to Cameroon? Hedi was not quite sure. She looked forward to it but was somewhat afraid as well. Over the years she had learned a lot about Africa, particularly Cameroon. She had received so many letters, heard so many stories and seen so many pictures. Now, everything no longer seemed out of reach.

The places seemed as familiar to her as if she'd been there a number of times herself. There were the bush churches and the villages, where Ernie and his helicopter had been welcomed with so much joy. There was the Moslem settlement where they were allowed to meet the chief, the *Lamido*, and enter into his court to meet his wives. They spent the night in a clay house while a thunderstorm beat down on them. They had an adventurous fondue meal. There was the singing of the natives. There were many flights across the never-ending jungle. She was able to relax and enjoy the lush green landscape and the lively cities. She learned what TIA meant: This is Africa!

Upon returning home, she found a way to put her newly-found impressions into words:

> God is more real and alive in Africa. He is closer and more tangible than in Europe. Why? The threat

of danger, whether from disease, animals or other human beings, is much greater. You must stay in prayer for protection at all times. When you take a drink of water, you pray it has been filtered. When you eat fondue, you hope no harm will come to you since you don't know whose dirty hands have just prepared your meal. When you walk through town, you pray that nobody will steal the clothes off your back. If you need a tool, you pray to find a store that sells it. Nothing can be taken for granted. Every day, the game is a new one: will you win or lose?

You learn what it means to cry out to God. When lightning hits your house, there is no insurance to cover it. If you are sick, there is no doctor close by. If you get robbed, no one will reimburse you. You have to start back at square one. Surviving is hard. You have to fight on every front. Nothing is simply dropped into your lap.

People walk everywhere. The streets are filled with pedestrians. One person might be taking fruit to the marketplace...or baskets...or eggs...or a chair. Everyone is trying to sell what he has just finished building. Either a buyer is found or else you have to march everything back home. Either there is enough food for you the next day or not.

Hardship can be felt everywhere. People submit to a seemingly unchangeable fate. You can see it reflected in the faces of adults and even the children. You can sense it in the air. Yet, I am amazed time and time again at their resolve. Curly heads balance broad straw platters filled with bags of corn upon them...or bundles of wood...or wooden beams...or bananas...here and there and everywhere. Through the streets and alleys they go—up and down the stairs and across bridges, through water, through the muck and mire and on and on....

Chapter 44

From Suffering to Victory

After the Africa trip, Ernie and Hedi tacked on a few days of relaxation to their vacation. They were in their beloved Italy. On the third day they were returning to the campsite after a short excursion. The man attending the gate said, "Telefonare Svizzera!" (*"Call Switzerland!"*) Hedi gave her husband a worried look. Something had happened, for certain. But it was late at night and there was no phone.

The next morning, Ernie headed for the office to make the call. It wasn't open yet. He was deeply upset as he paced back and forth, waiting to reach Trogen. Hedi sat in front of their tent concerned, expecting Ernie with news at any moment. Finally he returned. He wasn't smiling and looked pale as a sheet. He sat down next to her.

"What's up?"

"There was an accident in Ethiopia."

"With the helicopter?"

"Yes."

"Anybody hurt?"

"No. Both are dead."

"Who?"

"Steve and another missionary."

They could not get another word out. They felt paralyzed. Steve...Steve was no longer alive! Ernie remembered the days he had spent with him in Uganda. Only recently had he started working in Ethiopia. Helpful, friendly, experienced–that was how Ernie remembered him. Hedi could only think about Kathy, Steve's wife, who was still mourning her little son Colby. How was she going to survive this second blow?

Their tent neighbors looked over at them. They sensed something was not right.

"Come va?" ("How are you doing?")

Ernie replied, "Accidente con helicottero, due morti, due amici." *("An accident with the helicopter. Two friends have died.")*

It was good to talk to somebody, to have a reason to stand up and get moving.

"We're going home now. I need to go to Ethiopia and help Kathy!"

Never before had they dismantled the tent and loaded the car so quickly. They informed their friends in the village and out in the country and set off. It was a short, painful farewell. And back they went to the "battle set before them."

Already the next day, Ernie flew out to Addis. He was concerned about Kathy. He was surprised to see her so composed. She even insisted on accompanying him to the site of the accident. It was a small open valley with a ditch, some shrubs and trees. The assumption was that the engine of the helicopter had broken down as they tried to fly across this range of hills. Steve had probably tried to make an emergency landing. Both men had to have died as the helicopter first hit the ground. While Ernie and the specialists inspected the site, Kathy sat down at a distance and looked into the valley.

When Ernie came to take her back home, she said thoughtfully, "What a beautiful place to go home." Her husband Steve had not died: he had gone home. Where did Kathy get the strength to talk like that?

It had been a hard blow for the entire Helimission family—the pilots, their wives and children, the office staff in Trogen and Hedi and Ernie. Not just the rainbow-colored helicopter, almost new and only in use for a few months, had been totally wrecked. No, the loss of Steve, their missionary, pilot and friend, left a much more gaping hole.

Ernie took Kathy and her five-year-old son Steven back home with him to Switzerland. Upon greeting them,

Hedi remembered with a twinge how she had, only two years prior, embraced the entire family in welcome. And now? Half of the family was buried in Africa.

Kathy and Steven spent a few days in Trogen. The summer temperatures brought warmth to their hearts. Ernie took them for a walk on the beautiful island of Mainau, which was filled with gorgeous flowers.

"Ernie," Kathy started timidly, "my heart is in the mission. I know I can't fly, but I'd love to continue working for Helimission."

Ernie was surprised. He didn't answer immediately but thought for a moment.

"Isn't there anything I could do in America?" Kathy asked herself more than him. "Well, yes, I sure could visit churches and talk about Helimission. I've seen a lot of things and can talk out of firsthand experience."

This small, energetic woman had some good ideas. She refused to give in to her mourning.

"I've never seen this side of you, Kathy. You're a very brave gal. We'll do everything we can to support you."

Then she looked at Ernie for a long time. Finally, she said softly, "Maybe I'll be able to find you some pilots who would love to serve God and aren't afraid of danger. God is always looking for people ready to be used by Him, isn't He, Ernie?"

Chapter 45

Helimission in Action

"The work of this organization is controversial..." was a passage from a letter written to the organizer of a benefit concert for Helimission. Nothing could be truer. Yet, its efficiency...its results...and its meaning to recipients of aid more than justify the means. Most endeavors had been successful, but there had also been setbacks to cope with.

Our slogan, "Help from the Air Makes It There," is for real. People from all walks of life, from various countries and of different doctrines confirm that the help coming "from above" did not come in vain. People in Europe and the Western World utilize helicopters where everything is well-organized–and insured! Why shouldn't the machines be available in Africa in the areas where no one in their wildest dreams think help can come? Why is this? As repeated over and over again in this book, there are often neither roads nor public transport available. Seldom does someone have his own car.

Have we Westerners not often found ourselves "looking up for help" in certain situations? How many times did the circumstances seem impossible to us? When the help did arrive, it sparked something deep down within us–our belief in miracles. This is how people must have felt when the helicopters touched down, delivering food, water or vaccines. Above all, the choppers brought other people, men and women who could give more than just material goods. They brought comfort and strength, teaching and counsel, encouragement and joy.

Amidst all the happy events, there were a number of sleepless nights. There were times when wars erupted, and we had to withdraw from a country. Other times, flight permits were taken away and helicopters banned from flying. Sometimes, pilots gave up. All of these events give content and meaning to the vague term, "controversial."

Helimission, its pilots and staff must remain extremely mobile and flexible. In order to give you, my dear reader, some insight into what that means, let me offer a fitting example:

Our Second Mission to Albania, April 1992

April 24 – Ernie returns from Albania. "We've got to go back a second time. The people have no seed," he tells me. "Nothing's growing, and they'll be starving by next winter. My heart is so moved by the situation. I wouldn't be able to sleep if I didn't go back."

My reply was, "And I can't sleep if you do go back."

April 27 – We start organizing everything. We need seed potatoes, seed corn and fertilizer. Juerg and Tabea have been commissioned to locate a ferry, a truck and helpers.

April 28 – Ernie and I relax in Gandria for four days.

May 4 – We get back. Ernie learns that the ferry has not been booked. He calls around and finds out that all of them are booked out, apart from one ferry in Brindisi, Italy, going to Ingominitsa, Greece, on May 18. They had planned to take the ferry on May 15 to begin distributing goods on May 18. Time is running out. Now is planting time. Nevertheless, everything has to be postponed for three days.

In the meantime, Ernie finds seed potatoes in the Bern area of Switzerland. He manages to negotiate a price of twenty-five Swiss-Francs for 220 pounds. As a result of an interview with a Christian radio broadcaster, he receives an offer from Germany for seventeen Deutschmarks. He orders 100 tons. Switzerland doesn't allow him to cancel his order. Therefore, he buys fifty tons in Switzerland and fifty in Germany.

May 14 – Once again, we rent four trucks from Frederici. They drive around the Bern area to collect the potatoes and drive on to Germany. The following morning, they take care of customs matters before heading out for Brindisi, Italy via Austria and across Brenner Pass, a mountain pass in the Alps between Austria and Italy. They are carrying forty tons.

May 16 – Werner offers us his trailer again. On Saturday morning, Heinz the driver and Gerda the team cook, as well as Martin and Ralf from the Army base in Bueckeburg who will be helping with the flights, leave Trogen. The route they will follow is via San Bernardino, Rimini and Bari to Brindisi. At 8:30 Monday morning, they will pick up seven ferry tickets from Mr. Gavan in Bari, Italy.

May 17 – On Sunday morning Ruedi and Andreas leave Sepach for Brindisi in their Mercedes Jeep. They will be the drivers of the Volvo tank truck which is stationed in Brindisi temporarily. Both of them have a special license for driving hazardous goods. They will be driving the truck back to Tirana, Albania as well. The truck with trailer had departed Durres in Albania and had arrived in Bari, Italy, on April 24–with much stress and no preparation–that is, without any paperwork at all. In the meantime, the truck had been parked at Davide's church in Brindisi, waiting for its second mission. At least this place was fairly safe! The trailer contains a forklift, fuel canisters, water canisters, nets, food for the crew as well as all of the supplies needed at the depot in Tirana.

For the last couple of weeks, Ernie has been looking for seed corn and fertilizer in Italy. He gets two offers and takes the cheaper one. He rents a truck. Together with the others in the convoy, he wants to transport these eleven tons to Albania via Greece.

Late at night, my answering machine is blinking with a message. Thank God, the thing is working again. Ruedi has arrived in Brindisi with his Mercedes Jeep. It's rather unlikely that the Volvo will make it across the Italian border to Greece without getting a stamp from the customs office. Italy and Greece have an agreement making that illegal.

May 18 – Very early in the morning, Ernie calls Davide in Brindisi. Ruedi is to take the forklift out of the truck trailer and transfer it to the trailer of the Mercedes Jeep. That, however, is practically impossible because the forklift weighs two tons. Ernie asks everyone to take all the supplies for Albania out of the trailer and put them into the sleeper cabs of the trucks. If need be, they can at least start with the distribution in Albania. On Thursday, a ferry is crossing over from Bari to Albania. Maybe, by then, the Volvo will be allowed through customs. Three acquaintances from Brindisi drive to Bari to fight for a spot on the sold-out ferry boat. We expect to hear from them by 10 a.m.

10:15 a.m. – Ernie must leave for Tirana. We wait for a call–in vain. Tabea drives Ernie to St. Gallen to catch the train to Kloten.

10:50 a.m. – Mr. Gavan from the Anglo-Italian Shipping Company calls. He was the person who booked the ferry for us. He says things don't look good because the Volvo entered the country without proper paperwork. Without customs clearance, nothing can be unloaded. The goods are confiscated. The drivers could end up in prison for "contrebande," smuggling, that is. I get alarmed and immediately think of the BO in Chile. We go to the office, sit down at the desk and start praying. Ernie is on his way to Albania. Yet, we cling to the words, "When the need is greatest, God's help is nearest."

11:40 a.m. – Ernie calls me from the airport. I explain everything to him. At the same time, we get a call from Mr. Gavan in Bari. I hold the two receivers "face to face" and let Ernie speak with Mr. Gavan. Mr. Gavan has an idea: we should take the Volvo back to Bari because the paperwork needs to be stamped there. We should park it outside of the premises of the port.

"Go to Mr. X, who will help you to smuggle the Volvo into the port," he suggests. "Then, make sure you get your official stamp. Let's try that, Mr. Tanner."

Mr. Gavan is a Briton but knows a lot about the Italian way of doing things. He helps us tremendously.

"Leave everything in the Volvo," he warns. "Don't take anything out. It's too dangerous. We'll try to get everything on board the ship in Brindisi tonight."

2 p.m. – Ruedi calls from Brindisi. Tabea explains everything to him and says he should get in touch with Mr. Gavan immediately.

3:30 p.m. – I think Ruedi is on his way to Bari by now. God help him not to drive too fast! Muehlemann, Gasser, Erich and Ernie are on the plane going to Tirana. God help them not to lose their cool! I make myself a cup of coffee.

5:15 p.m. – Mr. Gavan is calling. The truck from Italy is at the customs office. It can't get through because there is no invoice for the load. There's nothing we can do on this side because we don't know where Rino bought the fertilizer and the corn. Rino is also on his way, headed toward the Volvo. We keep praying at the office.

6:15 p.m. – Mr. Gavan calls again. Tabea picks up the phone. She smiles and a look of relief crosses her face. First, the Volvo is back on its way to Brindisi after being cleared at the customs office. Secondly, the Frederici trucks have made it through customs as well and are ready to go on board the ferry boat. They had been in Brindisi, but we had been unable to radio them from Switzerland to let them know that they would have to go through customs first. Thirdly, a fax from the fertilizer company has confirmed the invoice for the goods aboard the Italian truck. It also received clearance from customs. (How long are the offices open down there, anyway?) Tabea, who's still on the phone, is about to shout hallelujah, praise the Lord!

By now, we are confident that the entire convoy will proceed past all other obstacles as well and make it to Tirana the following night.

P.S. It did arrive one day later–Wednesday at 6 p.m.!

The Helimission organization and its staff have to be mobile, flexible and adaptable. The pilots are continually on standby, ready to answer emergency calls. In case of political unrest, they have to be prepared to leave their respective countries. If need be, they may also have to take over a position in another country if one of the others goes on furlough. Sometimes, it means extending one's three-year contract or rescheduling one's own furlough.

At this date, there are only two countries where the original machines are still posted. The good old Ecureuil HB-XPN keeps making its route in Cameroon. Meanwhile in Kenya, people are still well-acquainted with the speedy Bell HB-XDY chopper. The XSH was put to use in Tanzania in 1989, but we were unable to secure a permanent flight permit. From time to time it was allowed to visit the swamps in the southern part of the country. This was done in connection with a missions organization based in Dar es Salaam. The long flight from Kenya was worth it. The reaction of the people there confirmed that every single time.

Ethiopia, the country which we had prayed for so much back in Trogen, has opened up wide for helicopter missions. Two machines are stationed there. The seven-bladed XSP stands ready in Addis Ababa to serve the high mountainous region to the north. The blue XSH is based in Arba Minch. The pilot needs it down there to reach the southern tribes. Despite the danger, he is really thrilled about the effectiveness of the flights which give him the opportunity to preach to thousands of people there. He also transports Ethiopian missionaries into the region.

On the large island of Madagascar out in the Indian Ocean, the seasons are directly opposite to ours. A lot of other things are upside down and the other way around, too! We have a chopper with Swiss registration there, the Ecureuil HB-XON. It was transferred from Kenya where it had remained more or less of a "sleeping beauty." As a result of hostile outbreaks in 1993 in Zaire, many Caucasians, missionaries included, were forced to leave the country. The XON also had to be removed from our base in Rwanguba and was then grounded in neighboring Kenya. Its "rude awakening" and adventurous flight to Madagascar are another vivid example of having to be "flexible"! Madagascar is another very poor and mountainous country. The pilots, missionaries and developmental aid volunteers working there have only one prayer: send us "laborers into the vineyard"!

For the time being, Albania was to be the final destination for the Bell HB-XLL after a long, long journey. After being dedicated to God's service in St. Gallen, it got sent to the Philippines in a container but made it no further than the port. Helimission was not willing to pay exorbitant customs duties; hence, the container returned without accomplishing a thing. Later, it crashed in Ethiopia, but its five passengers survived. Rebuilt in

New Zealand, it was, thereafter, employed in Papua, New Guinea. After its pilot returned home on the spur of the moment, the machine was packed up again. It was taken to Albania where it was used from 1992 to 1997. It has flown more hours than any of the other machines. Food, clothing, shoes, seed grain, Bibles and much more could be transported to the poorest of the poor living in the mountains. That helicopter has been, in every respect, fulfilling the statutes we laid down for the Helimission at the beginning.

Helimission celebrated its twentieth anniversary in Trogen in 1991. At that time, an action plan for earthquakes was presented. It included setting up emergency bases out of aluminum containers which could be easily transported as air cargo and then assembled at their destination. They could be equipped for use as an emergency medical station, kitchen or quarters for personnel. Water tanks, lavatories, and hydraulic tools for lifting heavy debris were also discussed for their feasibility. The missing puzzle piece was finding a high-powered helicopter to transport all of these things from any given airport to the disaster zone. There, they could be put into use immediately. With the acquisition of the Bell 412 in 1992, the puzzle was completed.

As early as April 1992, the Bell 412 was sent to Albania, where not a natural but rather a "political earthquake" wreaked havoc. The families of farmers in the remotest of valleys and mountains there were freezing and going hungry. The best means of aid could be supplied from the air. The Bell 412 with registration number HB-XVU passed the test. It was replaced by the XLL in the month of October and returned to Trogen. There, it remained ready to go at any time for future rescue missions. Unfortunately, governments of disaster-hit areas would often reject the help so readily available—with or without an explanation. Despite that, it remained on standby until 1994 when it got another chance to save the lives of refugees in Goma, Africa.

The Helimission crew is, today, just as much on standby, even if an uncertain future is staring them in the face. Its call is like the Good Samaritan's: to carry out acts of mercy wherever people are suffering from hunger and sickness...wherever there are refugees...wherever people are abandoned, helpless, in fear.

Of course, in this context, many possibilities must be questioned, for the entire world is full of misery. Where should we be helping? Who should be the first to receive help? Can a helicopter be used there? Does this possibility already exist? Is it worth it in this case? Isn't it just a drop in the bucket? What if those who were rescued become the victims of other brutal men later on? Can we ever expect a thank-you?

If you have ever seen multitudes suffering, you'll know that these questions become irrelevant. You won't ask if it makes sense or not or how much it all will cost. You'll simply roll up your sleeves and start helping. Those who haven't experienced such anguish firsthand–only getting news from the media–simply cannot grasp the great effort put forth and often small results accomplished. Help can't be measured in numbers. It's a matter of the heart. It's about loving your neighbor.

Wherever agony and despair bring darkness to places in the world, Helimission wants to help make the light of God's love shine by using helicopters to its advantage. Wherever people are crying out for help, we want to fly it in when no other way is possible. After all, "**Help from the air makes it there!**"

– # # # –

The HELIMISSION Foundation

CH-9043 Trogen, Switzerland

Telephone: ++41-71-343 7171

www.helimission.ch

Printed in the United States
52702LVS00001BD/1-105